Believe Celebrate Live Pray

BELIEVE
CELEBRATE
LIVE | PRAY

A WEEKLY WALK
WITH THE CATECHISM

JEM SULLIVAN, PH.D.

Our Sunday Visitor
Huntington, Indiana

Nihil Obstat
Msgr. Michael Heintz, Ph.D.
Censor Librorum

Imprimatur
✠ Kevin C. Rhoades
Bishop of Fort Wayne-South Bend
June 22, 2020

The *Nihil Obstat* and *Imprimatur* are official declarations that a book is free from doctrinal or moral error. It is not implied that those who have granted the *Nihil Obstat* and *Imprimatur* agree with the contents, opinions, or statements expressed.

Except where noted, the Scripture citations used in this work are taken from the New American Bible, revised edition © 2010, 1991, 1986, 1970 Confraternity of Christian Doctrine, Washington, D.C., and are used by permission of the copyright owner. All rights reserved. No part of the New American Bible may be reproduced in any form without permission in writing from the copyright owner.

Every reasonable effort has been made to determine copyright holders of excerpted materials and to secure permissions as needed. If any copyrighted materials have been inadvertently used in this work without proper credit being given in one form or another, please notify Our Sunday Visitor in writing so that future printings of this work may be corrected accordingly.

Our Sunday Visitor Publishing Division
Our Sunday Visitor, Inc.
200 Noll Plaza
Huntington, IN 46750
www.osv.com
1-800-348-2440

ISBN: 978-1-68192-183-9 (Inventory No. T1893)
1. RELIGION—Christian Life—Spiritual Growth.
2. RELIGION—Christianity—Catechisms.
3. RELIGION—Christianity—Catholic.

eISBN: 978-1-68192-184-6
LCCN: 2020942683

Cover and interior design: Chelsea Alt
Cover art: Creative Commons - CC by NC

PRINTED IN THE UNITED STATES OF AMERICA

To my parents, Donald and Josephine,
my first "living catechisms,"
this book is dedicated with deep gratitude.

For their words and actions that witnessed
daily to the transforming power of faith shared
in joy, perseverance, and fidelity to God.

For being the first to illustrate how lived faith,
as summarized in a catechism,
is a steady path to lifelong friendship with God.

"For (Wisdom) is an unfailing treasure; those who gain this treasure win the friendship of God."

— WISDOM 7:14

CONTENTS

Part VI — Conversion

Part VII — Forming the Good Habits of a Friend of God

Part VIII — The Word of God

Part IX — Friendship with God's People

Part X — The Church

Part XI — Mary: A Mother's Guide to Friendship with God

INTRODUCTION

For a journey to be successful, the traveler needs a dependable map, reliable directions, adequate supplies, and a trustworthy companion. The *Catechism of the Catholic Church* is all of these and more for a pilgrim on the journey of faith. This book is offered as a weekly guide, an accessible road map, and a spiritual companion to the *Catechism*. Here I hope to help you discover in the *Catechism* a treasured source for your growth in friendship with God. The *Catechism* is more than a written summary of Church doctrines and teachings; it is an invitation to discover the daily wisdom for life that permeates everything the Church believes, celebrates, lives, and prays.

I was a young, eager catechist and a student of catechetics when the *Catechism* was first published in 1992. It was presented to the universal Church as a "compendium of Catholic doctrine regarding faith and morals," a "sure norm for teaching the faith," an "instrument for ecclesial communion," a "support to ecumenical efforts," and a "sure and authentic reference text" for local catechisms and catechetical materials. Some thirty years later, it continues to serve these good aims.

The *Catechism*'s Prologue points to its primary audience of bishops and pastors, priests, catechists, and authors of catechetical texts. It notes that this universal expression of the "symphony of faith" will also be particularly useful reading for all the Christian faithful. The *Catechism* is thus offered to anyone who seeks an account of the hope that is in us (cf. 1 Pt 3:15) or looks to Christian faith for answers to the questions of life.

Whether you're familiar with the *Catechism* or not, this weekly companion offers you the opportunity to turn, or return, to it as a road map for your spiritual journey. Why accept this invitation? Because at the center of the *Catechism* is the person of Jesus Christ, who desires

11

your friendship! By his life, death, and resurrection, Jesus reconciled us to friendship with God in the power of the Holy Spirit within the community of the Church. "In reading the *Catechism of the Catholic Church*," Pope John Paul II said in his 1992 apostolic constitution, "we can perceive the wonderous unity of the mystery of God, his saving will, as well as the central place of Jesus Christ ... sent by the Father, made man in the womb of the Blessed Virgin Mary by the power of the Holy Spirit, to be our Savior. Having died and risen, Christ is always present in his Church, especially in the sacraments; he is the source of our faith, the model of Christian conduct, and the Teacher of our prayer" (*Fidei Depositum*, sec. 3).

Each chapter of this weekly retreat with the *Catechism* highlights one of the four "pillars," or parts, of the *Catechism*, arranged in a four-week cycle: The Profession of Faith (Creed), The Celebration of the Christian Mystery (Sacraments), Life in Christ (Ten Commandments and Beatitudes), and Christian Prayer (Our Father). You will find numerous suggestions for reading, reflecting, and journaling around these four sections of the *Catechism*.

To begin, I encourage you to identify which version of the *Catechism* text you will use, whether an edition in print or online (found on the Vatican or USCCB websites). Don't be intimidated by the number of pages or the formal language of the *Catechism*. As you travel through the fifty-two weeks of this retreat you will learn, study, and reflect on every section of the *Catechism of the Catholic Church*, in accessible, bite-sized portions.

You may opt to read one chapter each week for a full year, or read as many chapters at a time as you find helpful for your faith journey. You will gain the most benefit from this book if you set aside dedicated time each week to read, reflect, and record your learning and insights along the way. And be sure to have the Bible beside you as well, for "'Sacred Tradition and Sacred Scripture, then, are bound closely together ... both of them, flowing out from the same divine well-spring.' ... Each of them makes present and fruitful in the Church the mystery of Christ, who promised to remain with his own, 'always to the close of the age'" (CCC 80).

This book rests on a simple spiritual truth: God desires your friendship more than you can imagine! The whole of Scripture is witness to God's desire to accompany and reconcile humanity to himself. From this spiritual truth flows the reason, hope, and invitation of the book you hold in your hands. My hope is that as you learn, reflect on, and live the beliefs, liturgical celebrations, moral teachings, and forms of prayer of the Church, the *Catechism* will become a trusted spiritual companion on your faith journey — a journey made within the community of the friends of God, that is the Church. My prayer is that you will discover in the *Catechism* an inexhaustible source for lifelong growth in your friendship with God.

PART I

OUR SEARCH FOR GOD

WEEK 1
The Deepest Desires of Our Heart

Believe

To be human is to desire. From our waking moments to the day's end, our desires inspire and shape our thoughts and actions. To satisfy our most basic needs, we desire food, drink, shelter, and rest. On a deeper level, our desires move us to accomplish goals, to excel in a career or hobby, to pursue our life's dreams. Most importantly, we desire relationships. We seek to give and receive love. We stay plugged in so we will not miss a beat on the high-speed virtual superhighway swirling around us. (Just think of the many times you will turn to your phone to check Facebook or Twitter today!) Without realizing it, we give a lot of attention to our desires on a daily basis.

What about the desires of the spirit?

On life's journey, we search for so much — some things last, others simply pass. Yesterday's burning desire is replaced by today's must-have-now. Yet in the whirlwind of human desires, we often ignore the deepest desires of our heart. Our spiritual desires get crowded out or simply ignored. Am I aware that all the things I restlessly seek, great and small, point to a void in my heart — a void that can only be satisfied by God?

By taking this book in hand, you have already made a choice to let God be the one to satisfy the longings of your heart. You have taken the first step on your journey of friendship with God with the wisdom of the *Catechism*. This book is meant to help you take your relationship with

God to a new, deeper, more satisfying level. Here you can take a weekly miniretreat, with the wisdom of the *Catechism of the Catholic Church* as your guide. In this book you will find tools and insights to help you believe, celebrate, live, and pray more fully than ever before.

Trust that making this retreat with the *Catechism* will bear good fruit in your life. It doesn't matter if you are reading this book as a cradle Catholic well-versed in your faith, just starting out as a beginner, or returning to your faith after a time away. Wherever you are in your walk with God, rest assured that he will draw close to you as you seek to understand and live by the life-giving truths of the *Catechism*.

To be human is to desire God, consciously or unconsciously. We enter and leave the world with this spiritual yearning. Ultimately, whether or not this desire is fulfilled depends on us. Perhaps even more importantly, God desires us. It can seem too good to be true, but God desires your friendship, more than you know or imagine. An awareness of your deepest desires helps focus and redirect your gaze to God, who alone is the source and fulfillment of every good desire.

WALKING WITH THE *CATECHISM*

"The desire for God is written in the human heart, because man is created by God and for God; and God never ceases to draw man to himself. Only in God will he find the truth and happiness he never stops searching for." (27)

The *Catechism* invites us to look closely at our desires. Not as a navel-gazing exercise in self-indulgence or self-absorption, but as one of many steps on our path to friendship with God. This week, ask yourself: What are my heart's deepest desires? What desires inspire and guide my life?

Many saints came to a point in their lives when they had to admit to themselves that they were deeply dissatisfied with life and the things they were pursuing. All of us have times like that. The things we so desired yesterday no longer satisfy us today. Yet rather than bringing us down or leading to despair, realizing our dissatisfaction with life can become a moment of grace. This kind of "spiritual crisis," whether large or small, can be the very moment we turn, once again, to God as the only source of the happiness we long for.

The life of Saint Francis of Assisi is a good example. Saint Francis was born into a wealthy family in the hill town of Assisi in Umbria, Italy, in the year 1181 or 1182. His father was a wealthy merchant and his mother was of noble birth. Francis's family expected the young boy to continue the family business. In his youth, Francis was keen on enjoying the pleasures of life, spending his family's wealth on carefree and self-indulgent living. He was particularly drawn to the music of the medieval troubadours and the chivalrous life of the knights. Around the age of twenty, Francis was taken prisoner during a battle. After his release from prison, Francis suffered a prolonged illness, and during his illness and isolation he began reflecting on the emptiness of his life. A spiritual crisis followed, during which he turned to God in earnest, looking for meaning and purpose. Soon after, an encounter with a poor, disfigured leper in his hometown transformed his life.

After years of distraction and chasing down fleeting enjoyments, Francis felt the desire for God written deep in his searching heart. He abandoned his family's life of wealth and comfort to embrace a life of radical poverty in imitation of Jesus. Saint Francis of Assisi left a lasting, transformative impression on the Church through his life lived in friendship with God.

As you begin this journey through the *Catechism*, I encourage you to make a list of all the persons, relationships, and things that make up the desires of your heart — the ones that take up the most of your thought, attention, joy, and even worry. Your list might surprise you, as it holds up a mirror to your life, to your soul.

Identify the persons, relationships, and things that bring happiness, peace, and joy. Note those that bring dissatisfaction and restlessness, perhaps even pain. As you raise your heart and mind to God in prayer, bring your list with you. This is one way to take stock of your present situation in life, to become aware of where you are spiritually.

Drawing on the wisdom of the *Catechism*, entrust yourself in faith to the God who writes his love on your heart. This week, offer to God the persons, relationships, and things on your list. Make a conscious effort to be thankful for both the positive and the not-so-positive, because God promises and does bring good out of everything.

God writes straight, even with the crooked lines of our desires and our life.

Finally, thank God for drawing you to him on this journey of friendship. His grace will be sufficient for you. His power will be made perfect in you as awareness of your deepest desires leads you to rest in the origin and goal of your life — God.

MY JOURNAL
Read and reflect on Catechism *27–30.*

In your prayer time this week, take time to list the great and small desires of your heart. Bring those desires to God in prayer each day. Thank God for offering you his friendship, and ask him for the grace to place all your desires within your desire for him.

THE BLESSINGS OF GOD

CELEBRATE

There is a treasure hunter in all of us. We love to find a good deal, a bargain value, a priceless antique, or a long-lost family photo or heirloom, whether these show up in our attics and basements, at yard sales, discount stores, or in forgotten personal belongings. Perhaps that explains the ongoing popularity of television programs like the *Antiques Roadshow* or *American Pickers*.

Do we seek after and delight in finding spiritual treasure in the same way? Are we attentive to the blessings of God — visible and invisible? Where do I look to discover the abundant spiritual gifts that God pours into the world and into my life each day?

God desires our friendship. The whole of Sacred Scripture tells of God's search for humanity. God sent Jesus, his Son, into the world to restore us to friendship with him. Thanks to his sacrifice, all of us, with the help of the Holy Spirit, can indeed become friends of God — it just requires our daily response to his ongoing invitation.

Being alert to God's blessings in the ordinary and routine circumstances of daily life is a simple step to growing in friendship with God. A heart that is grateful to God is a heart that can draw close to God and remain close to him.

The busyness of life gives us little time to pause and turn our gaze to God. Habits of pessimism or negativity make it even more challenging to see God's blessings in each day. Yet this is precisely backward! Reflecting on and being thankful for God's gifts each day is what sustains and nourishes faith in difficult times.

What are your trials right now? Perhaps it is a difficult family relationship, the debilitating or sudden illness of a loved one, or the loss of employment. Waiting for the results of a medical test, praying for the return of a child to the practice of faith, hoping for employment in a tight job market — these and so many other cares, concerns, and worries often prevent us from recognizing God's blessings in the ordinary moments and routines of each day.

As you continue your journey of growing in friendship with God by reading the *Catechism*, focus this week on recalling and being grateful for specific blessings experienced in your life, in the past and in the present. The habit of recognizing and thanking God for particular blessings — great and small — is a sure way to grow in friendship with God. Discovering God's concrete blessings allows us to grow in joy, in hope, and in that peace that surpasses all understanding. It allows us to recognize that *everything* we have is gift. The next breath we are about to take is a gift. Life itself is a gift.

As we develop the habit of thanking God for every gift, even in the difficult and challenging times of life, we allow God to come close to us, to walk with us as our truest friend on the path of life through the good and bad times.

WALKING WITH THE *CATECHISM*

"From the beginning until the end of time the whole of God's work is a blessing. *From the liturgical poem of the first creation to the canticles of the heavenly Jerusalem, the inspired authors proclaim the plan of salvation as one vast divine blessing." (1079)*

I know a family that begins their suppers by sharing what each person is thankful for that day. Going around the table, each family member shares one person, event, or thing they are thankful to God for. This is a simple, consistent, and profound way to recognize God's blessings, even in the most ordinary experiences of the day. Ordinary persons, events, and things are where we encounter God — his forgiveness, mercy, and love — in simple, even surprising ways.

God is never outdone in generosity, and everything in creation tells of his immense goodness. The universe is not a random arrangement of molecules and matter. No, the world and all it contains — with its beauty, order, and design — comes from the hand of a generous, powerful, and wise Creator, a God who is rich in mercy and love.

How can we get in the habit of recognizing God's blessings all around us? One very powerful way is by praying the psalms each day (perhaps joining in the Divine Office of the Church, also known as the Liturgy of the Hours). The psalms are a powerful way for us to develop the habit of seeing and thanking God for his presence in the world and in our life.

The *Catechism* tells us that God's desire to create, redeem, and sustain us is one vast blessing. Your life, your family and loved ones, your parish, and community all participate in the unending blessings of God on the world. The more we practice gratitude for God's blessings, the more this gratitude becomes the lens through which we see the world.

Take the time this week to become aware of the many blessings of God in your life.

My Journal

Read and reflect on Catechism *1077–1083, 2626–2628, and 2637–2638.*

Take a few minutes each day of this week — perhaps right before you go to bed — to recall and thank God for one particular blessing you have experienced in the day. If for any reason you're having trouble finding blessings in your day, recall a blessing from your past. Jot down some concrete ways you can turn the attitude of gratitude into a lifelong and daily habit in your family, home, and personal life.

WEEK 3

GOD'S INVITATION OF LOVE

LIVE

To live as a friend of God rests on the "yes" we say in response to God's invitation of love. Our "yes" offered to God in faith becomes the most fundamental decision of our life, made not once, but over and over again in the day-to-day circumstances we face. How does our friendship with God shape our actions, decisions, and life itself?

Here we come face-to-face with a paradox of the Christian life. Saying "yes" to God means we may have to say "no" to certain ways of thinking, acting, living, and even some relationships that undermine the freedom, peace, and happiness God wants us to have. It turns out, many of our desires, even good ones, if not placed within our deepest desire for God, can leave us feeling empty and sad. Recognizing what we may need to say "no" to is not easy.

"Enter through the narrow gate," Jesus tells us. And he also warns, "How narrow the gate and constricted the road that leads to life. And those who find it are few" (Mt 7:13–14). These words of Jesus must have perplexed his disciples. For surely, he did not mean for the disciples to be narrow-minded, closed in, elite, or exclusive. Rather, Jesus' invitation to enter through the "narrow gate" reveals that freedom and truth are two sides of the same coin. God's grace frees a person *for* love born of truth. To choose the "narrow gate" is to let oneself be guided by truth that comes from God, the truth who is God, and the truth of who I am as a child of God. To fit through the narrow gate, we have to get rid of any excess baggage — that is, anything that takes our attention, desire, and energy away from the one thing that matters most. This is what it means to say "no" to certain things.

Ultimately, this "no" sets us free to say "yes" to God by entering the narrow gate. This is a "yes" to living in God's love and becoming his friend. Knowing that God desires my love, I am truly free to say "yes" to him in ever deeper ways. This is the "light bulb moment" in the spiritual life: when we recognize how fleeting is the alluring security of wealth, fame, pleasure, power, and acceptance by others.

If I find myself unhappy, restless, dissatisfied, and empty, could it be that my desires are aimed at the wrong things? I will not be happy until my will, my heart, and my mind rest in God, the only source and guarantee of true and eternal happiness.

WALKING WITH THE *CATECHISM*
"God put us in the world to know, to love, and to serve him, and so to come to paradise." (1721)

The third pillar of the *Catechism* is the Christian moral life lived as our response to God's love. Striving to live by the Ten Commandments and Christian moral principles is not a burdensome restriction on our freedom, nor does it demand blind obedience to rules and regulations imposed by religious institutions. By striving to live the Christian moral life, we respond to the desire for happiness that God has placed in each of our hearts. The moral teachings of the Church are the sure path to genuine happiness, true freedom, and liberating virtue by which we respond to God's love. We live by God's commands because we love God.

The lives of Christian saints are powerful reminders that genuine human happiness is to be found in God alone. The saints are like works of art, God's masterpieces, who show us the truth that "true happiness is not found in riches or well-being, in human fame or power, or in any human achievement ... but in God alone" (1723).

Take the example of Saint Augustine (AD 354–430), bishop, Doctor of the Church, and master of the spiritual life, who wrote of his spiritual journey in his *Confessions*. Augustine's classic spiritual autobiography is a must-read for anyone serious about the spiritual life. Every human journey of friendship with God will find some echo in Augustine's moving journey from doubt to faith.

From a young age, Augustine showed great promise with intellectual gifts and a charismatic personality that would set him on a path of worldly success, wealth, fame, and prestige. But the moral decisions he made and the choices that dominated his life left him deeply unsatisfied. Despite his many detours — spiritual, moral, and intellectual — the driving search for truth was the one constant of his young life. He was far away from God, yet God was close to him in ways he did not even know or understand.

As Augustine eventually discovered, to decide *for* God is to decide *against* ways of life that deny God's love and will — and only this choice can lead to lasting fulfillment and joy. What we most desire and want in life is as important as what we do not want.

This week, challenge yourself to say "yes" to what pleases God by saying "no" to the things that long experience has taught you will only leave you empty.

MY JOURNAL
Read and reflect on Catechism *1720–1724.*

List the things you have desired and wanted that ultimately proved unsatisfying. How have these things led you away from God's love and mercy? Pick one thing on that list, and ask God for the grace to continue to say "yes" to him by saying "no" to that thing, whatever it may be.

WEEK 4

OUR DESIRE FOR GOD

PRAY

In one of many poignant scenes in *Ben-Hur* (the award-winning 1959 epic), the movie's main character, Judah, a Jewish prince, encounters Jesus for the first time. Judah has just been falsely accused of the attempted murder of a Roman governor and sentenced to life imprisonment as a slave in the Roman galleys. As he stumbles along a dusty road, bound in chains and exhausted from the heat of the day, he reaches for a drink of water. A Roman soldier stops him from quenching his thirst by taking the water and spitting it in his face, with a cruel lash of his whip.

Thirsty and beaten to the ground, Judah raises his bowed head only to encounter Jesus, who offers him a drink of water. Jesus' look of love encourages Judah to persevere in his trial. Toward the end of the movie, as Jesus walks his way of the cross to Calvary, Judah breaks through the crowds to return the act of loving kindness by offering Jesus a cup of water. For Jesus had quenched not only Judah's physical thirst, but his deep spiritual thirst for God's love.

Human desires are like physical thirst that wells up in us from time to time. Our daily desires direct our actions, decisions, and relationships. Our desire for God, however, is a mysterious, insatiable thirst that only God satisfies. We return, time and time again, to awareness of this deep desire for God.

The amazing thing is, our thirst for God is a response (and nothing in comparison) to God's thirst for us. Yes, God *thirsts* for you and me. This is such a liberating truth of the spiritual life! God desires our

27

friendship before we are even aware of our desire for God. God's desire for each of us is magnificent, beautiful, and limitless.

How can we know that God desires our friendship? We discover the beautiful, profound truth that God first seeks us and desires to be in communion with us when we pray. When we turn to God in prayer, whether in silence or in formal or informal words, we discover that God is there first, thirsting for our love and friendship.

WALKING WITH THE CATECHISM

"It is he who first seeks us and asks us for a drink. Jesus thirsts; his asking arises from the depths of God's desire for us." (2560)

To be a friend of God is to be a person of prayer. The fourth pillar of the *Catechism* is Christian prayer. The faith that we hold and profess in the words of the Creed, celebrate in the sacraments, and live in the moral life grows in our personal relationship with the living and true God.

In the weeks to come, we will learn about models of prayer in Scripture, forms and kinds of prayer, overcoming distractions and obstacles to prayer, and the prayer that Jesus teaches us: the Lord's Prayer (or "Our Father").

This week, our reflection on Christian prayer is based on the Gospel story of Jesus' encounter with the Samaritan woman at the well (cf. Jn 4:4–42). Jesus meets a Samaritan woman who comes alone to the village well to draw water at noon, the hottest time of day. She is lonely, an outcast whose life situation has ostracized her from her community, to the point that she goes to draw water when no one else will be there. She is rightly surprised when Jesus approaches her and begins speaking to her.

Jesus asks the Samaritan woman for a drink of water, knowing well that some of her life choices have led to exploitation and isolation. Jesus does not add to her pain and loneliness by judging or condemning her. Rather, he thirsts for her conversion, a change of life that will restore her dignity as a child of God and reconcile her to friendship with God and the community.

Then Jesus tells her who he is and that he wants to give her living water. Wells, although they are a vital source of water, contain only stagnant water, symbolic of the heavy emptiness the woman feels as a result of her choices.

Jesus promises the Samaritan woman a different kind of water: "Whoever drinks the water I shall give will never thirst; the water I shall give will become in him a spring of water welling up to eternal life" (Jn 4:14). Jesus promises the woman life-giving water that will quench her deepest thirst for God.

Jesus promises you the same. What wells have you drawn from that have left you thirsty, disappointed, burdened, isolated, and empty? Will you drink the life-giving waters that wash away sin and restore and strengthen us with new life in friendship with God and neighbor?

The *Catechism* invites us to accept Jesus' thirst for our friendship. Let God find you ready to abandon stagnant waters in exchange for the deeply satisfying waters of divine grace in God's word and in the sacraments of the Church.

My Journal
Read and reflect on Catechism *2560–2561.*

After you read the *Catechism*, read John 4:4–42, the Gospel account of Jesus' encounter with the Samaritan woman. Jesus thirsted for her, and he thirsts for your friendship as well. This week, make a note of the concrete ways you will continue to accept Jesus' offer of the life-giving waters of his love and mercy. Let God find you wherever you are in the spiritual life, and let him love you.

PART II

GOD COMES TO MEET US

WEEK 5

CREATED *IN* AND *FOR* LOVE

BELIEVE

God loves you, and his first act of love was to create you and give you a share in divine love as the ultimate meaning and purpose of your life. So far on our journey with the *Catechism*, we've been reflecting on friendship with God and God's desire for our friendship. This week we return to one of the fundamentals of Christian faith: the belief that God exists and that he creates us in love for an extraordinary purpose, as recounted in the opening chapters of Genesis.

Have you ever tried watching a 3D movie or IMAX film without 3D glasses? Chances are you gave up watching the movie pretty quickly. Without 3D glasses, the film appears grainy, the figures blurry. The action seems disconnected and meaningless. The biblical book of Genesis is like a 3D lens that lets us see the universe and the meaning of our own existence. It invites us to think of creation not as one belief among other equally interesting notions about God, but as the truth of where we come from and what we were created for. Viewing reality through this lens allows us to see the world and ourselves clearly, filled with the meaning and purpose God intended for our lives.

What we believe about creation affects us at the most fundamental level of our being. And what the Church invites us to believe about creation is more awe-inspiring than the most breathtaking natural wonder of the world, for it brings us face-to-face with a personal and loving God, who is also the creator and sustainer of all that exists.

The Bible offers an astonishing worldview of the origin, meaning, and final purpose of creation. This understanding of the created world is so astounding in its beauty and reasonableness that it must be either mysteriously true or a very elaborate and fantastical fairy tale. In faith, we receive the Christian understanding of creation as a gift; we believe it to be true, and we experience it as true because it corresponds to our heart's deepest longing to be loved unconditionally and eternally. God is the Divine Artist whose masterpiece is the entire universe and each and every creature.

God's purpose in creating you and me was nothing less than our good — he wants our good simply for our sake. To will the good of another for the sake of the other is the very definition of love, as Saint Thomas Aquinas tells us. And this divine love is the origin of our existence and the reason we draw breath every moment of our life. God's love and friendship is the purpose, the meaning, and the final goal of our creation and existence.

As Pope Benedict XVI told a group of young people in September 2010, "God wants your friendship. And once you enter into friendship with God, everything in your life begins to change." If you doubt that God desires your friendship, try looking with the lens of faith at your origins. God created you because he loves you, because he wanted to shower you with love — and he wants you to discover the meaning and purpose he has for your life.

WALKING WITH THE CATECHISM

"Creation is the foundation of 'all God's saving plans.'" (280)

"With creation, God does not abandon his creatures to themselves. He not only gives them being and existence, but also, and at every moment, upholds and sustains them in being, enables them to act and brings them to their final end." (301)

The *Catechism* helps us see creation as God intends and reveals. Creation comes from the hand of the Trinity: the Father, Son, and Holy Spirit. The life-giving love of the Divine Family spills out into the created world, the universe, the natural order, and each of us, created in God's image and likeness. Saint Thomas Aquinas put it this way: "'Creatures came into existence when the key of love opened [God's] hand'" (293).

Then, as if divine love were not enough reason for the creation of the world, God made us to be his sons and daughters through Jesus Christ in the power of the Holy Spirit. This high calling is the purpose and meaning of every human life — to share in God's being, wisdom, and goodness here on earth and for all eternity. Reclaiming our original dignity as children of God, the dignity we lost by sin, becomes a reality as we grow in friendship with God. We are not the product of some vague, impersonal force of necessity, of blind fate or chance, a random combination of molecules that come from and go to nowhere. We receive life as pure gift — God's gift.

After he creates, God does not abandon his creatures to themselves. At every moment, God sustains and upholds his creatures in being. He blesses human beings in a special way with free will and intellect to know and love him and to be good stewards of the created works of his hands.

The *Catechism*'s teaching on creation offers us a consequential choice: We can believe in an impersonal force who is somehow at the origin of the universe, nature, and our being but is indifferent to our existence, development, and livelihood. Or we can believe in a personal God who loved us into existence and whose love continues to sustain the universe, the order of nature, and every breath we take.

Sure, the world is not perfect, nature can be terrifyingly destructive, and life is often filled with difficulties, disappointments, and pain. But these imperfections are part of our common and fallen human condition. They are the opposite of what God originally intended when he created the universe and each one of us out of love. Every limitation in creation and in human life is precisely where we encounter the merciful hand of God, who over and over again restores, heals, and brings us back to friendship with him.

MY JOURNAL
Read and reflect on Catechism *301–308.*

Begin each day of this week with a prayer, however brief, acknowledging God as creator and sustainer of your being. Thank God for his grace, and for the wonderful plan and purpose he has for your life. Begin each day by placing yourself, everything you are, everything you will do, and everything you hope to achieve into the hands of God. Take time to write down specific circumstances, events, and persons that reveal God's saving plan to love you and sustain you in existence.

WEEK 6

SACRAMENTS: TANGIBLE SIGNS OF GOD'S LOVE

CELEBRATE

At the beginning of the animated movie *Up*, a brief montage of images captures the lifelong relationship of Carl and Ellie, the husband and wife who are among the film's main characters. Their life story begins with the happy days of their childhood friendship, their wedding, and settling into their new home, and it continues through the many ups and downs of their life together. The young couple sets out to save money for a travel adventure. But as time goes on, they must spend their savings on more immediate and pressing needs. They grow old and gray together with a love and devotion that deepens with the passage of time. Eventually, Carl decides to buy tickets for their long-hoped-for adventure, even as Ellie's strength begins to diminish with sickness and old age. Their desire for a grand travel adventure together remains unfulfilled. In the final scene, Ellie, now on her sickbed, closes her book of adventure, the symbol of her life. Then she holds Carl's hand as he bids her farewell with a gentle kiss on her forehead. Not a word is spoken between them, but the tangible expressions and concrete gestures of love from these animated fictional characters are real and moving.

We give and receive love, gratitude, pride, and loyalty through concrete actions and signs. It is not enough to simply say "thank you," "I love you," "I'm here by your side," or "I am proud of you." We recognize love, gratitude, pride, and joy through visible expressions and tangible gestures. Children show gratitude to parents, spouses express sacrificial love for one another, parents voice concern for a child's well-being, and friends convey commitment and loyalty in tangible words, perceptible gestures, and concrete acts of good will.

God speaks to us and walks with us in the same way. Jesus, the Son of God incarnate, stands at the heart of God's communication with the world. In sending his only Son, God stepped into our bodily reality, showing us how to live and love just as he created us: as a unity of body and spirit. Because we are bodily creatures, we express and perceive spiritual realities through words, gestures, signs, and symbols. That's why Jesus left us the sacraments: These signs, drawn from the created world, convey to us God's friendship, love, and mercy.

Reflect on the concrete actions and gestures by which you share and receive love, mercy, kindness, and hospitality from the people you encounter in your daily life. In a similar way, God's love, healing care, forgiveness, and mercy are present in our lives in so many tangible ways. In a particular way, the sacraments are God's unique way of drawing us into friendship with him and sustaining us in that relationship.

WALKING WITH THE CATECHISM

"The purpose of the sacraments is to sanctify men, to build up the Body of Christ and, finally, to give worship to God. ... They not only presuppose faith, but by words and objects they also nourish, strengthen, and express it." (1123)

Human beings mark the passage of time with celebrations of birthdays and anniversaries, speeches and memorials. Such celebratory and commemorative moments are opportunities to express in concrete words and gestures many intangible human thoughts and feelings — love, admiration, loss, and praise. We send and receive cards and gifts, and we find ways to rejoice in the accomplishments of others with honors, medals, trophies, and other forms of tribute. As time passes, these celebrations form a "memory bank" that capture the deep meaning of our most cherished human relationships.

Our relationship to God is a friendship. God is not an abstract, obscure force we must somehow discover by means of human cleverness. Nor is God to be known by an elite few through a series of intricate puzzles and ingenious riddles. The God who revealed himself in Jesus Christ in the power of the Holy Spirit desires our personal friendship. God comes in search of us in love. How do we know this? God's desire to be reconciled with humanity was so strong and deep that he sent his only Son, Jesus, into the world. Jesus' life, death, and resurrection are the divine outpourings of God's healing and reconciling love into the world. And when Jesus' earthly life was over, he assured his disciples, and us, that he would remain with us always.

The seven sacraments of the Church are the privileged means by which Jesus remains close to us, bringing divine healing and mercy. In the sacraments, God comes closer to us than we are to ourselves! The sacraments are not ritual obligations that we fulfill as baptized Christians. The sacraments are the means by which God's divine life and love flow in and through our lives. When we approach in faith and receive the sacraments, we are lifted up out of this fallen human condition and made holy so that we can become members of the Body of Christ, a graced community of faith that transforms the world with the love of God.

To participate in the sacramental life of the Church is to exercise our most profound vocation: to become sons and daughters of God who stand humbly with inalienable dignity and worth before him as we offer our whole life in praise and worship, thanksgiving and joy.

Just as we express love, joy, and admiration in our everyday relationships, the sacraments are the means, instituted by Jesus, by which our faith is nourished, strengthened, and transformed in the light of God's radiant love. In the sacraments God expresses divine joy that we are truly his friends!

MY JOURNAL

Read and reflect on Catechism *1123.*

List concrete ways — words, gestures, actions — in which you experience the love and friendship of the people in your life. Can the same be applied to God? How is God revealed in your life through concrete circumstances, situations, events, and persons? How is God present and active in your life in the sacraments of the Church? Do you go to meet him there?

WEEK 7

FRIENDSHIP WITH GOD

LIVE

Friendship with God and neighbor is the whole point of human existence, from beginning to end. Jesus makes this plain throughout the Gospels, where his many relationships teach us what friendship with God should look like.

In the tenth chapter of the Gospel of Luke, Jesus enters a village where a woman named Martha welcomes him (cf. Lk 10:38–42). Her sister, Mary, sits close to Jesus at his feet, listening attentively to his words. In frustration, Martha, burdened and distracted with multiple tasks of hospitality, comes to Jesus and says, "Lord, do you not care that my sister has left me by myself to do the serving? Tell her to help me" (Lk 10:40).

Jesus responds with powerful words: "Martha, Martha, you are anxious and worried about many things. There is need of only one thing. Mary has chosen the better part and it will not be taken from her" (Lk 10:41–42).

Notice that Jesus listens to Martha's complaint. He is a true friend, willing to hear patiently her burdens and concerns. Then, as a true friend, Jesus speaks plainly, from his heart. He challenges Martha's understanding of true hospitality, beyond multitasking with its endless distractions and demands. To truly welcome him into her home, Martha needs first and foremost to encounter Jesus personally, to grow in communion with him through attentive listening. Being a friend of Jesus is more fundamental than doing many tasks, however necessary. Active service to Jesus needs to be rooted in silent contemplation of his presence and his words.

Commentators on this gospel story often highlight the contrast between the active life of Martha and the contemplative stance of Mary, as Jesus clearly points to contemplation as the better part. The seventeenth-century Dutch painter Johannes Vermeer captured this gospel scene in a famous painting, completed around 1656 (used as the cover of this book). In Vermeer's composition, we see Jesus, Mary, and Martha grouped closely around a table. Mary sits at the feet of Jesus, listening in rapt attention. With her head resting on one hand, her side profile invites us to share in her perspective. Vermeer invites us to see ourselves as taking part in her silent listening to the words of Jesus.

Vermeer paints Martha in motion as she enters the room, bringing to the table both a basket of food and her concerns about her sister's lack of help. The basket contains a freshly baked loaf of bread. Perhaps Vermeer is offering a Eucharistic reference here, as he reminds us of the necessity of silent contemplation of God's living word, present and active in the Eucharist. It is only in silence that we grow in what Pope Saint John Paul II calls "Eucharistic 'amazement' " at the gift and wonder of Jesus' Real Presence in the Blessed Sacrament (*Ecclesia de Eucharistia*, 6).

Jesus sits on an ornate wooden chair with an arm rest, a seat typically reserved for figures of authority and prestige in Vermeer's day. Jesus' haloed head turns to Martha in response to her anguished concerns, while his right hand extends out to Mary, appreciating the one who chose the better part.

Vermeer places Jesus in the heart of an intimate scene of family relationships. By entering their home, Jesus enters into the intimacy of their family life and relationships. To emphasize their bonds of friendship, Vermeer paints the three figures of Jesus, Mary, and Martha close together, as if enclosed in an imaginary circle. In the warm light that floods this interior setting, Jesus teaches these two sisters, and us, the importance of listening to his life-giving words as the path to true friendship with him.

WALKING WITH THE *CATECHISM*
"Endowed with 'a spiritual and immortal' soul, the human person is 'the only creature on earth that God has willed for its own sake.' From his conception, he is destined for eternal beatitude." (1703)

God's creating us is itself an act of divine friendship — one for which no one, however saintly, can ever express adequate thanksgiving. We are the only creatures willed by God for our own sake. In creating us and endowing us with a "spiritual and immortal" soul, God wants nothing other than our good, our well-being, our happiness. We are loved unconditionally into existence. We are the only creatures with the capacity to contemplate God and to live in relationship with him. What a gift of faith!

The *Catechism* tells us, "The first man was not only created good, but was also established in friendship with his Creator" (374). For "God created man in his image and established him in his friendship. A spiritual creature, man can live this friendship only in free submission to God" (396).

The eternal community of divine friends is the Trinity of Father, Son, and Holy Spirit. Their divine friendship spills out into the world. God's desire for friendship with creation is fulfilled perfectly in the sending of his own beloved Son, Jesus Christ. In Jesus' life, death, and resurrection, the divine offer of friendship is extended to you and to me.

Just as he chose to enter the home of his friends Martha and Mary, Jesus desires to enter our homes and to journey with us. Will he find a hospitable welcome in our home, in our family relationships, in our hearts, and in our lives? Will he find us listening attentively to his words so that our actions flow from knowing and believing we were created for eternal happiness?

Christian life is a paradox. We long for happiness, choose the way of God's commands, and strive to become saints in this life. But our entire existence is oriented to one goal, one purpose, one meaning: eternal life and friendship with God. Our earthly life is not the only nor the most important reality. Our life comes from God and looks toward God's eternal communion and friendship. By living as God's friends here and now, we are able to taste a little bit of heaven here on earth.

My Journal

Read and reflect on Catechism *1703, 1730.*

Set aside thirty minutes this week to read and reflect on Luke 10:38–42, and spend some time pondering Vermeer's painting, *Christ in the House of Martha and Mary*. In prayer, thank God for the gift of being loved into existence. Note one spiritual practice you will begin or renew to help nourish and grow your friendship with God, a daily reminder of the eternal purpose and goal of your life.

WEEK 8

First Steps in Prayer

Pray

First steps are usually marked by joyful celebrations. Parents remember with delight their baby's first steps and first words. We remember as milestones landing our first job, owning and driving our first car, and buying our first home.

As astronauts Neil Armstrong and Edwin "Buzz" Aldrin made their historic landing on the moon on July 20, 1969, Armstrong famously described their first steps as a "giant leap for mankind." What was unknown to the world at the time was how one of the astronauts chose to celebrate the event as they waited to take their first steps into history.

In his memoir, *Magnificent Desolation,* Aldrin recounted that after the lunar module had landed safely on the moon and before they took their first steps, he radioed to earth, requesting for a few moments of silence. He invited "each person listening in, wherever and whomever they may be, to pause for a moment and contemplate the events of the past few hours, and to give thanks in his or her own way." Then, during those few moments of pause, Aldrin read silently the Gospel words he had written on a small card: "I am the vine, you are the branches. Whoever remains in me, and I in him, will bear much fruit; for you can do nothing without me."

Aldrin then took out a miniature chalice, bread, and wine from his personal allowance pouch. As he recounted in a 1970 article, "I poured the wine into the chalice our church had given me. In the one-sixth gravity of the moon the wine curled slowly and gracefully up the side of the cup. It was interesting to think that the very first liquid ever poured on the moon, and the first food eaten there, were communion elements."

Millions around the world watched the historic first human steps on the moon. But few knew of Aldrin's personal marking of the event, kept secret out of respect for NASA's request to astronauts to refrain from overtly religious comments and to keep their public remarks general. Years later, Aldrin admitted, "At the time I could think of no better way to acknowledge the enormity of the Apollo 11 experience than by giving thanks to God." At this and other significant moments of great human achievements, the human heart instinctively turns heavenward, to God.

Prayer is the first step in the sincere movement of the human heart to God. When we pray, we come to God, but God is always there first, full of love and fidelity, overflowing with mercies that never end. God's initiative of love always exists before any first step we take to him in prayer.

WALKING WITH THE CATECHISM

"In prayer, the faithful God's initiative of love always comes first; our own first step is always a response." (2567)

The *Catechism* offers the "why" of Christian prayer before it describes the "when" or "how to." There's a lot of wisdom in beginning this way. Understanding why the Church prays helps us feel less intimidated by and more drawn to prayer. We move from fear or indifference to a desire to pray that wells up in the heart. Fears and concerns about how to pray, or being daunted or overwhelmed by various methods and forms of Christian prayer, slowly dissolve once we grasp why the Church prays.

The *Catechism* tells us that prayer is our response of love to God's love that always exists first and in abundance beyond imagining. God's love is the reason we pray. It's that simple.

Prayer is my gaze of love on God, returning God's gaze of love on me.

When we understand prayer as our response to God's faithful initiative of love, we slowly become less afraid, less hesitant, and less sluggish in prayer. We even begin to long for moments of prayer, however brief, hurried, or scattered. Times of prayer will not be perfect, especially not right away. But we grow in confidence to approach God in prayer when we know that the one who first waits for us waits with unconditional love, divine mercy, and relentless forgiveness. Our first small, hesitant steps to God in prayer are always preceded by God's enormous steps of love. How do we know that he is coming to us first? Because we see his love revealed fully in the redeeming life, death, and resurrection of Jesus. By creating and redeeming each of us, God has taken the initiative to be in friendship with us.

Whatever our steps in prayer might be — however small or big — we never forget that God's initiative of love always comes first. Every step closer to God in prayer is our response to God's first step of love toward the world and toward us. We can do nothing, even pray, without God first loving us into existence and sustaining our every breath.

MY JOURNAL
Read and reflect on Catechism *2567.*

Make a note of first steps in your life that you are proud of. Then, list first steps you have taken or want to take in the spiritual life. Thank God for his constant love, and for continually inviting you to deeper friendship with him. Even this prayer of thanksgiving is a response to God's initiative of love. Ask God to fill you with ever greater love in response to his immense love for you. Ask God for the gift of prayer.

PART III

ACCEPTING GOD'S OFFER OF FRIENDSHIP

WEEK 9

SEEKING GOD

BELIEVE

It is never too early or too late to become a friend of God. Take the example of Abraham. He heard God's call to leave his home for the new land of Canaan, not knowing where he was to go. Then Abraham and his wife, Sarah, who was barren, were given the promise of descendants as countless as the stars of the sky. When Abraham first heard these promises of God, he was seventy-five years old! (Read the full biblical account in Genesis 12:1–9.)

The author of Genesis notes simply that Abraham did as the Lord directed him, and he believed what the Lord promised. Abraham trusted God. He walked by faith. And he was blessed as God walked with him every step of the way. Faith opened the way for Abraham to have a profound relationship with God.

Events, persons, relationships, and circumstances of life invite and challenge us to walk by faith in God. We find ourselves asking, "Can I really know God? Can I be God's friend?" These questions are not merely a matter of intellectual inquiry or abstract speculation reserved for philosophers, theologians, and scholars. These are questions that touch the heart of who we are and who we were created to be — friends of God.

Years ago, I taught theology to high school senior boys (and I lived to tell the tale!). The questions they posed during classroom discussions were thought-provoking. Early in the semester, one young man declared he was agnostic. When pressed for an explanation of his position, he claimed neither faith nor disbelief. He was convinced that nothing is known or can be known of the existence or nature of God. Nothing beyond the material, quantifiable, measurable world could be known with certainty. His beliefs could be summarized in this way: "I cannot know God and there are no absolute truths. You have your truth and I have mine. I decide what counts as truth and no one can tell me this or that is true!"

Sounds like a typical, idealistic teen, you might say. But in fact, a good number of adults today live out that same attitude. Many hold that there are no objective truths and that human beings cannot really know anything beyond what is scientifically measured and verified. Truth, if there is such a thing, is reduced simply to private feelings and opinions, personal impulses and desires. By this measure, I am the sole judge of what is true and what is not.

This way of thinking, admittedly easy to fall into, is filled with inner contradictions and negative consequences. For instance, the assertion that there are no objective truths is self-contradictory. If there is no objective truth, then the very statement "there is no truth" cannot be objectively true. Reducing truth to personal opinions and feelings puts me in a corner, in the trap of self-reliance that leads nowhere. Living in a self-enclosed reality without reference to God has many consequences that lead down the road of dissatisfaction, disillusionment, and emptiness.

We did not create ourselves, and we cannot give ourselves meaning and purpose. Our human life does not contain within itself the first principle or final end of our existence. The meaning and goal of our life must be received as sheer gift from the one who created us. Only in God, who created us out of love, will we discover the divine origin, dignity, meaning, and goal of our lives.

WALKING WITH THE *CATECHISM*

"The person who seeks God discovers certain ways of coming to know him. These are also called proofs for the existence of God, not in the sense of proofs in the natural sciences, but rather in the sense of 'converging and convincing arguments,' which allow us to attain certainty about the truth." (31)

When God created us in his image, he gave us reason. Our capacity for reason helps us to know God. With this divine gift, we can know God with certainty, based on evidence offered by the created world. So reason is not an enemy of faith, as many argue: It is an invaluable aid to faith. This is why the Christian tradition speaks of "proofs" for God's existence, available to human reason.

If you find yourself debating the existence and nature of God, chances are the first thing that needs to be clarified is what we mean by the word "God." God is not one being among many, and thinking of him as such is a sure path to confusion, doubt, and contradiction.

God is the first principle and final goal of all that exists, says the *Catechism*. This means that God is not one being among others, a quantifiable being we can choose to believe in or not. Rather, God is being itself. This means he is also love itself, truth itself, and goodness itself. The mystery of who God is transcends any limit, boundary, or measurable constraint that emerges in the human mind. God is *ipsum esse* (in the words of Saint Thomas Aquinas), which is to say, the act of being itself.

Think of it this way. Everything that exists has a cause for coming into existence, meaning something else outside of itself brought it into being. We were brought into this world by our parents, for example. If the universe began to exist, as science posits, then something else caused it to come into existence. God, on the other hand, has no cause. Nothing and no one else brought him into being. God simply is, without cause, and he is the life-giving font of all that is.

When we speak of "proofs" for God's existence, we are not talking about proofs in the natural sciences, verifiable through observation, experimentation, and scientific methods. Rather, "proofs" for God's existence are converging, self-evident arguments that point our natural reason with certainty to God. These "proofs" for the existence of God are two-fold: the natural world and the human person. The *Catechism* sums up these "proofs" or arguments for God's existence in paragraphs 31–35.

Saint Thomas Aquinas is best known for exploring and explaining these approaches to God. His contributions to theology were immensely consequential for Christian thought. Aquinas argues that movement, change, contingency, and the world's order and beauty are all starting points for coming to know God. The human person's openness to truth and beauty, moral goodness, freedom and the voice of conscience, our longing for the infinite and for happiness — these are all signs of our spiritual soul, which can only have its origin in God.

Reason gives us confidence to know that God exists and to understand who God is. But God reveals himself and gives us grace to welcome his revelation in the act of faith. And faith and reason are not incompatible. Both are God-given paths for us to come to know and love God.

Faith is a lifelong adventure leading us out of ourselves to God. Supernatural faith — faith that God exists and that he is who he says he is — is a gift from God, one received at baptism and strengthened through prayer and the sacraments. To travel the path of faith is an exhilarating, not always easy, journey of discovering our true identity, our dignity, our purpose, and our final rest in God. Responding to the invitation of faith leads us to the truth of God and the truth of who we are in relationship to God, the Creator and Redeemer of the world. On the journey of faith, we become truly free and truly human. By faith, we walk the same exhilarating path of Abraham and of every saint in the Christian tradition. Living by faith, we become friends of God.

MY JOURNAL
Read and reflect on Catechism 31–35.

This week, as you ponder the question, "Can I really know and be a friend of God?," reflect on Abraham's faith in Genesis 12 and 13. Note three elements of your faith that can be inspired by Abraham's faith. Make a note of ways you image God. Then read the *Catechism* sections noted above. Thank God for the gift of reason. Reflect on how God's gift of reason helps you to know and love God. Each day this week, ask God in prayer for the gift of faith.

WEEK 10

THE "SIGN" OF CREATION

CELEBRATE

Even if we live by faith, we often miss or overlook God's call to friendship in our daily life and surroundings. The reality is that God speaks to us through all of creation. "The world is charged with the grandeur of God," wrote Gerard Manley Hopkins, an English Jesuit poet. But do we see and hear God's grandeur in the world around us?

Think of the number of times in one day that we check our social media pages, our text messages, our email messages, or the latest trending news. We live in the so-called Age of Information. At no other time in history have human beings communicated and shared information and news so rapidly, across distances, languages, and cultures. Anything we want or need to know can be reached in real time with a few clicks. Whether we like it or not, we are all, at one time or another, harried passengers on this high-speed information superhighway.

What we come to know through the ever-expanding global digital realm is information about the world and our relationships. No doubt the spread of the Gospel in our time is advanced by the prudent use of new and effective means of communication. But no matter how sophisticated, efficient, and accelerated our communications and media technology become, we cannot depend on our use of them to deepen our personal friendship with God. The constant demand that screens make on our time and psychological energy can leave us distracted, exhausted, and drained.

Why? Because the constant noise of our communication makes it nearly impossible for us to hear God's voice in our hearts and in the world around us. The Holy Spirit, dwelling and active in us, wants to open our eyes, our hearts, and our minds to the many beautiful traces of our Creator that surround us in our daily lives. Yet we cannot see or hear the divine action of the Holy Spirit if we're constantly distracted.

To be Catholic is to see the world as "charged with the grandeur of God." It is to see creation through a sacramental lens, not as the product of random and indifferent chance or as a series of molecular accidents, but as a true "sacrament" — a sign — of divine design, beauty, and order. Nothing created by God simply ends in itself or can be reduced to utilitarian profit. The created world is one immense "signpost" pointing the eyes and ears of our hearts back to God. From this truth comes ecological awareness of our responsibility to be good stewards of creation.

This week, practice taking time, even just small moments, to look up and away from screens to see creation. Seek to approach everything and everyone with the eyes of faith, and experience the world, creation, and other people as gifts from God.

WALKING WITH THE *CATECHISM*

"God speaks to man through the visible creation. The material cosmos is so presented to man's intelligence that he can read there traces of its Creator. Light and darkness, wind and fire, water and earth, the tree and its fruit speak of God and symbolize both his greatness and his nearness." (1147)

The *Catechism* invites us to develop a sacramental imagination. This means the habit or practice of seeing the world as God sees it: radiant, transparent, and overflowing with divine love, power, and nearness. To develop this imagination, we have to purify the inner gaze of our hearts and minds so we can see the world as God sees it. Only with a sacramental imagination can we truly grow in friendship with God.

The opposite of a sacramental imagination is a "throwaway culture," a mind set that objectifies persons, creation, and things, seeing them as replaceable, temporary, and disposable. To develop a sacramental imagination is to purify our habits that prevent us from seeing the beauty of creation and the sacred dignity of each human person. It requires that we put aside old ways of seeing the world and other people as mere objects to use and discard, or as disposable means to our personal ambition or self-indulgent pleasures.

Saint Augustine, as the *Catechism* tells us, wrote: "Question the beauty of the earth, question the beauty of the sea, question the beauty of the air distending and diffusing itself, question the beauty of the sky … question all these realities. All respond: 'See, we are beautiful.' Their beauty is a profession [*confessio*]. These beauties are subject to change. Who made them if not the Beautiful One [*Pulcher*] who is not subject to change?" (32).

Take time this week to practice Saint Augustine's exercise. Look around at the created world and question the beauty of what you see, from a tiny leaf to the vast cosmos itself. Think of your favorite landscape or place of natural wonder, such as the Grand Canyon or Yosemite. Reflect on the beauty and sacredness of human life that comes from the creative, loving hand of God. What is my responsibility in the face of the gift of creation?

Allow the Holy Spirit to transfigure your sight and hearing so that your heart and mind can overflow with gratitude for the creative power and closeness of God's grandeur.

MY JOURNAL
Read and reflect on Catechism *1145–1152.*

If you can, pray the words found in Daniel 3:56–88 each day this week. This canticle of praise for God's creation focuses our hearts and minds on God's presence and power revealed in the order, design, and beauty of the natural world. Make a list of those elements of the natural world that speak of God's power, beauty, and presence to you personally. Commit to one concrete habit that will help you spend less time looking at screens and more time listening to the voice and call of God, who speaks through the wonder and beauty of creation.

WEEK 11
"I AM A SINNER"

LIVE

"I am a sinner. This is the most accurate definition. It is not a figure of speech, a literary genre. I am a sinner," Pope Francis said in 2013, in response to a journalist's question, "Who is Jorge Mario Bergoglio?"

"I am a sinner." These words of Pope Francis bring into focus the theme of our reflection this week: the reality of sin and human separation from God. Ask yourself: How would I answer the question of my identity — who am I? Would I give the same response as Pope Francis?

If we doubt that the human condition is sinful, we need only look at the day's headline news. War, violence, addiction, oppression, greed, and injustice are just some of the daily reminders that something is "not right" with humanity. We are plagued by our own impatience, unkindness, lack of compassion, and other sinful habits, great and small. In society, culture, family, work, and the daily network of human relationships that make up the journey of life, we know and experience personally the reality of alienation and sin. Left to ourselves, we human beings are "off balance" in our relationship with God, with one another, and with creation. The symptoms and consequences of our fundamental imbalance are to be found everywhere on a global, national, cultural, and personal scale. Human weakness and alienation weigh heavily on history and on each of our lives.

Most often, human sinfulness is explained away. We prefer to think that what is not right with the world is nothing but the result of psychological weakness, developmental flaws, or the necessary outcome of inadequate social, economic, and political structures. It's always someone else's fault! At the end of the day, this understanding of human alienation is unsatisfying because it is self-enclosed and circular. It assumes that acts and events of human sinfulness can be explained away by other acts and events of human sinfulness. And it presupposes that the remedy for human alienation is to be found in the human condition itself.

We circle around without ever coming face-to-face with the reality of sin. And because we don't come face-to-face with this reality, we cannot come to the joyful realization that all that is "not right" with the world has been overcome once and for all. The result is that we remain stuck in alienation and hopelessness.

The Bible and the Christian tradition offer a different understanding and response to human sinfulness. Rather than explaining away or excusing the reality of sin, the biblical worldview looks at sin through the lens of God's creation and original plan for humanity. We break through the self-enclosed circle of explaining sin away and into the bright light of God, the Creator and Redeemer of the world. Looking with eyes of faith, we see the truth and reality of human sinfulness in the light of God's plan and desire for our friendship.

God's grace can overcome all that is "not right" in the world and in us. Christ has already won the victory over sin. This is the source of our hope.

Acknowledging that each of us is a sinner and a member of the sinful human race is the necessary first step in friendship with God. Without this first step, our identity and our relationship to God will be illusory and superficial. A great weight is lifted off our shoulders when we begin to see that each of us stands in need of God's grace and mercy every day and every moment of life. The world does not contain within it the remedy for its alienation, weakness, and sinfulness; that remedy is found only in God. We cannot become friends of God until we can say, "I am a sinner."

WALKING WITH THE *CATECHISM*

"Man's freedom is limited and fallible. In fact, man failed. He freely sinned. By refusing God's plan of love, he deceived himself and became a slave to sin. This first alienation engendered a multitude of others. From

its outset, human history attests the wretchedness and oppression born of
the human heart in consequence of the abuse of freedom." (1739)

"To try to understand what sin is, one must first recognize *the profound*
relation of man to God, for only in this relationship is the evil of sin
unmasked in its true identity as humanity's rejection of God and opposition to him," says the *Catechism* (386).

Our relationship to God is the most profound truth at the core of our
existence. We were created to be in relationship, in friendship, with God.

Sin is a negation, a closing off, a turning away from, a refusal of God's
offer of friendship. It is turning inward to the will and pleasures that satisfy the self and moving away from God and the joy of living life as a gift
of self to others. No psychological, social, economic, or political reasons
can adequately explain this refusal to live as a friend of God.

When archaeologists unearth remnants of ancient civilizations and
cultures, they are delighted to find fragments of human remains, build-
ings, tools, pottery, art, and writing. From these fragments, they can
reconstruct how entire cultures and peoples lived, thought, communicated, and flourished in the past.

Our deep desires for peace, harmony, and unity are like archaeolog-
ical fragments embedded deep within us, remnants of our original human condition. God originally created us to live in harmony with God,
with our very selves, with others, and with creation. This perfect harmony was our common original purpose and destiny.

"Where are you?" This is the first question that God posed to Adam
and Eve as they hid in the garden after eating of the forbidden fruit (cf.
Gn 3:9). Yet God, being God, knew exactly where Adam was. This was
not a question about physical location. Rather, God was asking a spiritual
question: "Where are you in relation to me?" Put differently, "Why have
you moved away from friendship with me to alienation and sin?"

Genuine friendship is freely offered and freely received. Rather
than forcing friendship, God endowed his creatures with free will, the
freedom to choose to live in original unity and justice as his beloved
children. Our first parents chose freely to disobey God's command,
believing instead the lie that God did not love them but wanted domination and control. Our first parents were seduced by the tempter's lie,
"You will be like gods" (Gn 3:5). As a result, sin — personal and social

— continues in every age. In our lives, we are constantly faced with the temptation of Adam and Eve to refuse divine love and friendship and to live in the illusion that we are God.

Do I recognize the reality of sin in the world, and in my relationships, decisions, and life? Can I truly say, "I am a sinner!" with hope in God's mercy and love?

MY JOURNAL
Read and reflect on Genesis 3 and Catechism *385–390.*

The first three chapters of Genesis express in biblical language and narrative the truths of creation: its origin and end in God; its order and goodness; the vocation of humans, created male and female in God's image; the drama of sin; and the hope of salvation and reconciliation with God in the life, death, and resurrection of Jesus Christ. Reflect on the need to recognize the reality of sin as a refusal of God's offer of friendship. Write down concrete ways to move from refusing God's love to accepting and flourishing in the light and love of divine friendship. Thank God for creating you in love, and for the divine plan of salvation in Jesus Christ by which sin is overcome and humanity is reconciled to God.

WEEK 12

COMMITMENT TO PRAYER

PRAY

To choose God and reject sin requires daily effort, and in particular, a conscious commitment to prayer. Have you ever had a day when everything was a battle? When you struggled against the alarm clock; got stuck in traffic; rushed from one meeting or task to another; drowned in overcommitment to activities; faced dreary weather; fought through seasonal colds and flus; wrangled with the annoying habits of a friend, relative, or coworker; or simply fumed over missing papers or keys? The list could go on and on. We've all had such days, though hopefully they are few and far between.

When God created the world and human beings, he intended his creatures to live in union with him and with one another. The created order was meant to exist in harmony with itself and with God. Friendship with God was our original vocation. We were to live in the sure knowledge of who God is and who we are — creatures loved and sustained in existence by God.

Adam and Eve refused God's friendship. They fell prey to the original lie that God did not really love them and that they did not need God for their happiness. They refused God's offer of friendship, and this is what we call Original Sin. The consequence of their original refusal of God's love was a radical change in the human condition and creation. Now life itself is a battle. After the Fall, the human condition and creation became a battleground, a place of endless, tiresome, and at times frightful struggle against the consequences of alienation from God. Our friendship with God was replaced with alienation and isolation, felt deep within us and all around us in the created world.

The order and beauty of creation was our original inheritance. Now, instead, disorder and fragmentation are the rule of the day. Read the daily headline news if you doubt it. We were meant to live in friendship with God and one another, in childlike trust, awe, gratitude, and wonder. Instead, distrust, indifference, and even hostile disdain for God arise and gather strength in human hearts.

As we persist on our journey, the *Catechism* shows us a sure path to reclaim our friendship with God: the path of Christian prayer. Some of us may be taking the first steps on the path of prayer. Others may be continuing on a lifelong journey of prayer, marked by periods of intensity or laxity, joy, indifference, or neglect. Wherever you find yourself on the path of prayer, take this week to reflect on the place of prayer in your life and its power to restore you to friendship with God. Recommit to daily prayer.

WALKING WITH THE *CATECHISM*
"The 'spiritual battle' of the Christian's new life is inseparable from the battle of prayer." (2725)

The *Catechism* speaks of the "battle of prayer" as an inescapable part of the "spiritual battle" of the Christian life. But what is prayer? And what are some practical ways to find that joy and peace we long for and that God so desires to give us even in the experience of the "battle of prayer"?

The life of prayer, says the *Catechism*, is the habit of being in the presence of the Triune God in friendship, trust, and gratitude (see 2565). "Whether we realize it or not," says the *Catechism*, "prayer is the encounter of God's thirst with ours. God thirsts that we may thirst for him" (2560). What makes our prayer Christian is that we seek to be in communion with Jesus Christ and journey together with the Church, which is his Body (2565). We follow the example of Jesus, who prayed to his heavenly Father in times of joy, gratitude, and anguish. Our prayer to God can take on so many forms suited to each day's joys and challenges — blessing and adoration, petition, intercession, thanksgiving, and praise. All our personal prayer leads us to the public prayer of the Church, the Eucharist, which is the source and summit of the Christian life.

While prayer is deeply personal, it unites us visibly and invisibly with the communion of the Church and the communion of the saints. We are never alone when we pray. The whole Church, on earth and in heaven, prays with us. What power comes from such prayer!

Life requires that we give priority to many responsibilities, tasks, and challenges. The fast-paced world of social media can leave us stressed, harried, and overwhelmed. All the more reason to give priority to a consistent program of daily prayer that allows time for reflection, closeness to God's word, and communion with God. Times of prayer, however brief and hurried, become refreshing moments to break out of our cares and self-absorption into the bright light of God's peace and grace.

Prayer requires human effort. But the primary work in prayer belongs to God. Give God a chance to speak to your heart every day, to manifest his love in your life, to inspire you with wisdom for life's decisions. Give God a chance to restore your friendship with him by giving prayer a chance.

MY JOURNAL
Read and reflect on Catechism *2558–2565 and 2725.*

Create a prayer plan that can become part of your daily life, whether it's ten minutes or half an hour each day. Take some time to learn about the different forms and rich traditions of Christian prayer developed over centuries, time-tested by generations of the faithful. Seek forms of prayer that suit your schedule and where you are in your walk with God. These might include the Liturgy of the Hours, the Rosary, *lectio divina* (meditative reading of Sacred Scripture), and contemplative prayer. Most of all, make a decision this week to embark upon or continue your personal journey of prayer. Your friendship with God depends on it!

PART IV

THE GLORY OF GOD: THE HUMAN PERSON FULLY ALIVE

MADE IN GOD'S IMAGE

BELIEVE

What does it mean to be made in the image of God? It means being a "someone," not just a "something." It means being capable of freely giving of ourselves. Often, those who suffer inhumanity at the hands of others teach us powerful lessons about what it means to be human, made in the image and likeness of God.

Take the witness of Saint Josephine Bakhita, who as a child was kidnapped and sold into slavery in Sudan. Born in 1869 in a small village in Darfur, Sudan, the young girl was abducted while working in the fields with her family and then sold into slavery soon after. Trafficked from one cruel slave owner to another, the young Josephine endured unspeakable and dehumanizing psychological violence and physical torture at the hands of her captors. After being sold several times, she traveled with her new master's family to Italy to accompany their daughter to a school in Venice, run by the Canossian Sisters.

There, she heard the healing word of God and was confirmed in her undeniable dignity and self-worth as a child of God. When the Italian family sought to return to their business home in Sudan, Bakhita refused to follow. Thanks to caring interventions by the religious superior of the Canossian community and the cardinal of Venice, Bakhita's case was brought before an Italian court. A dramatic court ruling declared she had never been a legal slave, since the British had persuaded Sudan to outlaw slavery, and slavery was also outlawed in Italy. Bakhita had found faith and freedom!

Soon after, Bakhita decided to enter the Canossian community and made her religious profession in 1896. From then on, she dedicated the rest of her life to serving her religious community and to sharing God's love as the source of the dignity and worth of each human life. Her life was a testament to the Christian truth that even when our dignity is diminished by others, we are not just "something" but remain a "someone," precious and loved because we are nothing less than the image and likeness of God.

The question of the dignity and worth of human life has engaged generations of theologians, philosophers, scientists, doctors, and many others. It is an especially important question among people of faith. And while public debates are important and consequential, the Christian view of the human person is unchanging. We are made in the divine image and likeness with the capacity to know and love God and one another through our gift of self. No person, ideology, or political system can take away this image of God, imprinted deep in our very being.

The *Catechism* tells us that "catechesis on creation is of major importance" (282). In other words, what we believe about God's creation of the world and each human person fundamentally orients how we relate to God and to one another. To believe that God is the origin of our existence, dignity, and worth brings us to the heart of the meaning and purpose of life itself, understood as a divine gift. So, as we continue our journey with the *Catechism*, we are invited to reflect this week on the gift of being made in God's image and likeness. And we are challenged to strive to live up to our high calling of growing each day in the divine image and likeness in which we were created. We take up our responsibility to see others as God sees each one of the creatures he loved into existence. The good and the peace of our families, communities, and society depend on it.

WALKING WITH THE *CATECHISM*

"Being in the image of God the human individual … is not just something, but someone. He is capable of self-knowledge, of self-possession and of freely giving himself and entering into communion with other persons." (357)

The teachings of the *Catechism* on creation respond to the deepest human questions: "What is our origin?" "Where do we come from?" "Where are we going?" "What is our end and destiny?"

Answers to these fundamental human questions can be found by the light of human reason. Faith confirms and enlightens our minds so that we can more easily discover the truth that the world was created, out of nothing, by the loving word of God. We are not accidents of history or biology, mere products of random molecular combinations. Each human person is created in the image and likeness of God, loved into existence, and sustained by God's grace. Our innate dignity, worth, and capacity for love and service express this divine image.

The Christian view of the creation of the human person has profound consequences for individuals, communities, and society. To accept in faith and profess in the Creed that God is the origin, Creator, and Sustainer of each human person is the basis for a truly just, peaceful, and humane society. So we take the time this week to reflect on the gift of our creation by a loving God. In the sure knowledge of being loved into existence, we discover our self-worth, and we open our hearts and minds to giving ourselves to others in service, which lifts up the dignity of all people.

My Journal
Read and reflect on Catechism *356–361.*

List concrete ways — such as racism, human trafficking, and pornography — that the God-given dignity of the human person in our communities and in society is undermined or even denied. Then reflect on how the Christian view of creation, as explored in the *Catechism*, responds to the dehumanization of the human person in those instances. Make a list of actions and habits you can practice to affirm the dignity of others in a way that reflects the Christian view of the human person.

WEEK 14
The New Life of Divine Grace

Celebrate

What does it mean to be made new?

Caravaggio's paintings inspire us with their evocative light and ethereal shadows. In his *The Calling of Saint Matthew*, the Baroque master evokes the action of God's grace that makes all things new. As Jesus calls Matthew to be his disciple, he is making him into a new creation, portrayed by the artist's dramatic use of light and shadow.

Completed around 1600, the painting was commissioned for the Contarelli Chapel in the Church of San Luigi dei Francesi in Rome, where it can be seen today. The gospel event is depicted in the most ordinary setting of a small, darkened room. We are reminded that Jesus called his disciples as they went about the humble tasks and challenges of daily life. This is where we too are made a new creation as we experience God's call to friendship and healing presence in ordinary moments of daily life.

Caravaggio depicts Matthew seated among a group of men at a small table. Jesus and the apostle Peter, as we see them, have just entered the room on the right side of the painting. The men are startled by the appearance of Jesus, whose right hand points in a commanding yet loving gesture of invitation. The bearded figure, believed to be the tax collector, points to himself in dismay as if to say, "Me?" In his characteristic style, Caravaggio captures something of the spiritual drama that is unfolding across areas of bright light and deep shadow. Known as the technique of *chiaroscuro,* the sharp contrast of light and darkness serves not only to illuminate the scene but also to evoke the re-creation of Matthew that is taking place at this profound moment.

A beam of warm light radiating from the figure of Jesus brightens the darkened space of the cold room. This artistic use of light evokes what happens when we are made a new creation in Christ: When we hear Christ's call of friendship and respond with our entire lives in faith, the darkness of alienation, despair, and sin is overcome by the light of God's love. Every vocation to Christian discipleship is a call to receive and to live the gift of new life in Christ, in dramatic moments of conversion or in the ordinary events of the day. It is also an invitation to follow Jesus on the way of the Cross, prefigured in the cross-shaped window panel in the painting.

Art commentators are quick to note the similarity between the gesture of Caravaggio's Jesus as he points to Matthew and the iconic gesture of God as he awakens Adam to life in Michelangelo's ceiling frescoes in the Sistine Chapel. Here, one master artist pays homage to another.

The same God, creator of all that exists, who gave life to Adam, gives new life to Matthew the tax collector. This new life of divine grace is open to each one of us, too. Just as God's mercy makes all things new in Matthew's life, it can do the same in our lives, if we are open to this divine re-creation. It begins at our baptism and continues through every stage of life when we draw close to God in friendship.

Hopefully we will experience again and again in our walk with God the desire to be made anew. When the hurried pace of life, with its joys and challenges, leaves us overwhelmed, drained, and worn out, we long for a fresh start, a renewing moment, a new lease on daily life.

God offers us his word and the sacraments of the Church as the means by which we can be made new in Jesus Christ, each and every day. This invitation of grace is the most life-changing experience of being made anew in God. Will we respond in faith?

WALKING WITH THE *CATECHISM*
"Holy Baptism is the basis of the whole Christian life. ... Through Baptism we are freed from sin and reborn as sons of God; we become members of Christ, are incorporated into the Church and made sharers in her mission." (1213)

The word "vocation," from the Latin *vocare*, means "to call." By virtue of our baptism, each and every one of us has been given a new name. Baptism bestows on us the dignity and the call to live as a child of God, a new creation in Christ, and a temple of the Holy Spirit. Our common Christian vocation takes further shape in the particular call of our individual state in life.

The *Catechism* teaches us that baptism is the sacrament of regeneration through water and God's word. Only God can satisfy our deepest desires of heart and mind. Baptism gives us the gift we so long for — a new life of friendship with God, lived in the strength of divine grace. The waters of baptism symbolize our dying and rising to new life as a new creature. We do not earn this gift of new life. Rather, we receive new life in God with humility, gratitude, and faith.

This week, take time to reflect on the new life deeply longed for in every human heart. Bring before God all those persons and events in your life that need the new life of divine grace. Recall the gift of your baptism when you were called away from the darkness of sin into the light of friendship with God. Give thanks to God for the gift of your baptism, and for his constantly making all things new. Because of his mercy, we are sons and daughters of God, made new creations in Jesus (cf. 2 Cor 5:17).

My Journal
Read and reflect on Catechism *1213, 1265–1266.*

Thank God for the gift of your baptism and call on those graces to continue to renew your life today. Reflect on the gift of faith received at baptism and what that gift of faith means to you today. If it has been a long time, avail yourself of the Sacrament of Confession to restore the life of grace you first received in baptism. If you can, find out when your baptism occurred and mark that date on your calendar.

WEEK 15

LIVING IN FREEDOM

LIVE

Throughout the Scriptures, we see that God remains close to the people he called into covenant relationship. God made himself known at various times, in small and big ways, in ordinary and extraordinary events that shaped the people's history (cf. Heb 1:1). Still, the people of Israel often wondered if God was truly with them. From time to time they probably asked, "How do we know that God truly walks with us? Is God really present with us as a people and as individuals?"

Their questions can be ours as well. The human condition, with its joys and difficulties, its achievements and failures, can lead us to ask, "Does God walk with us? How can we be sure that God is present among us?"

In the fourth chapter of Deuteronomy, we hear the answer that Moses gives to the people of Israel as he assures them of God's unconditional love and constant presence among them. That answer may surprise us. For Moses reminds the people of Israel that God is close to them in the Commandments he gave them. The Commandments are thus an expression of God's love, a sure sign of God's presence among the people.

This understanding of the Commandments runs counter to the way we tend to see God's laws. How often do we hear it said that the Ten Commandments are simply a list of "do's" and "don'ts" that take the fun out of life? The message we hear everywhere, repeatedly, is that the Church's moral teachings, rooted in the Commandments, limit our freedom and restrict our full human flourishing. In this view, to follow the Commandments of God is to be less free, less enlightened, less human.

71

Jesus tells his disciples that he came to fulfill, not abolish, the law (cf. Mt 5:17). And Jesus promises that "whoever obeys and teaches these commandments will be called greatest in the kingdom of heaven" (Mt 5:19). In other words, God's commandments are not harsh burdens or strict rules we follow blindly that take the joy from life. Rather, to follow the Commandments is to be conformed to Jesus himself. What a gift that is!

Through faith, we know that God's commands correspond to our deepest human desires for love, peace, justice, and mercy. God's commands are not meant to restrict our freedom, to make us less free or less human. Rather, we are most free when we freely choose the good that comes from God. By following God's commands, we become truly free to love others as God loves.

Every one of God's laws corresponds to our natural desire for happiness. God places his divine law in our hearts in order to draw us close to him. For God is the one who alone fulfills the deepest desires of every human heart.

As you continue your journey with the *Catechism* this week, reflect on your approach to God's Commandments. Do you see them as limiting your freedom? Or do you see the Commandments as paths of life that empower you to be truly free for love?

Walking with the *Catechism*

"Freedom is the power, rooted in reason and will, to act or not to act, to do this or that, and so to perform deliberate actions on one's own responsibility." (1731)

"The more one does what is good, the freer one becomes. There is no true freedom except in the service of what is good and just." (1733)

The *Catechism* presents us with a profound truth: the more one does what is good in keeping with God's commands, the freer one becomes. Freedom is not license to do whatever I want to do. Rather, freedom is the exercise of a power, rooted in reason and will, to choose the good.

Understanding the nature and exercise of genuine freedom as a gift from God is one of the challenges of growing in maturity of faith and life. If freedom refers only to my own exercise of rights, then I will not be able to see how my freedom is at the service of the common good. The *Catechism* offers much wisdom to guide how we understand and exercise freedom so that it reflects our own dignity and that of others. Love and truth are the anchors of freedom, giving direction and ultimate purpose to the exercise of my freedom.

Along life's journey we become attached to things, ideas, and habits. Over many years, these attachments can make us less free, less able to choose the good of others and the way of self-giving love. These unhealthy attachments bind us to patterns of thought and action that are destructive to our dignity and to our relationships.

Our God-given freedom is meant to liberate us from attachments that harm us in body and spirit. God's gift of freedom removes the chains that bind us so that Jesus Christ can make us a new creation in him.

This week, reflect on whether you are truly free to love God and neighbor. Take stock of the habits and things that are like chains preventing you from experiencing the true freedom that God desires for you. Seek to live in the freedom of friendship with God.

MY JOURNAL

Read and reflect on Catechism *1731–1738.*

Honestly assess your own understanding of freedom. Reflect on whether you see your freedom as license or as the power to choose the good. Name one attachment that's still holding you back from living and loving fully in the light of God's commandments. Bring that attachment to God in prayer this week, asking God to help you overcome it. Ask for the grace to choose the good so that you may be truly free.

WEEK 16

A CONVERSATION OF
THE HEART

PRAY

Several years ago, I served as a docent at a major art museum in Washington, D.C. As I led groups through the museum's masterpiece collections, I had some interesting and thought-provoking conversations with visitors. One such conversation stands out in my mind. We were standing in front of a Renaissance masterpiece from the mid-fifteenth century, by the renowned Florentine painter Fra Angelico. As I spoke about the history and symbols of the painting, a middle-aged woman began to speak animatedly about the work. She talked about the meaning of its symbols and what they meant to her personally. In a few minutes, she had practically taken over the tour! It was wonderful to see this visitor enjoying the artistic treasures of the museum so much.

After the tour, I struck up a conversation with her. She told me she was born and raised in a Catholic family, but that during her time in college, and as her career unfolded, she fell away from the Church. She had always loved art as a child, so she decided as an adult that, instead of going to Mass on Sunday, she would visit the city's art museums for inspiration. On those weekly visits she was drawn to masterpieces with Christian themes. In her experience, sacred masterpieces helped to center her thoughts and brought her a sense of inner peace.

The story ends well in that she had recently returned to the practice of faith in the community of the Church. She credited for her return to the Church, among many things, the treasures of sacred art that drew her to contemplate the mysteries of faith in visual form.

We live in a distracted, hurried, and often fragmented world. As we go about our busy days filled with many responsibilities and challenges, it's easy to forget prayer, or to relegate it to a few moments here and there. Yet in reality, prayer is our lifeline to God. We learn to access and make use of this lifeline in and through the Church.

The Church has a rich tradition of prayer in vocal, meditative, and contemplative forms. All forms of Christian prayer have a single purpose: to bring us into friendship with God and to sustain us in that relationship. For prayer is a conversation of the heart with God who so desires our friendship that he sent his Son, the living Word of God, to speak the divine word of mercy, forgiveness, and love to the world. All forms and ways of Christian prayer have a single purpose: to bring us to and sustain us in friendship with God.

Over two-thousand years of the Christian tradition, rich and various forms of prayer have developed. Yet we know how difficult it is to keep to a consistent time of prayer and reflection on God's word.

WALKING WITH THE *CATECHISM*

"Christian Tradition has retained three major expressions of prayer: vocal, meditative, and contemplative. They have one basic trait in common: composure of heart." (2699)

We learn to pray by praying. And all forms of Christian prayer are paths to friendship with God. When we set aside time in our day, even brief and hurried moments, to turn our hearts and minds to God, we experience the presence and wisdom of God in our life. As Saint Thérèse of Lisieux once wrote, "For me, prayer is a surge of the heart; it is a simple look turned toward heaven, it is a cry of recognition and of love, embracing both trial and joy" (2558).

The *Catechism* tells us that the Holy Spirit teaches us how to pray. We simply place ourselves in the presence of God and his holy Word, and we open our hearts and minds to the inspiration of the Holy Spirit. We should search for the form of prayer that best suits our personality, schedule, and the responsibilities of our vocation. This week is a good time to begin that journey of discovering the form of prayer that fits us best in our current state of life.

In Christian prayer, we grow in a relationship with God, who is love. We move away from self-love, self-absorption, and self-reliance and move closer to God, the origin and source of our being and the one who sustains us in existence. Only in God do we understand who we truly are and the great dignity and worth we truly have.

MY JOURNAL
Read and reflect on Catechism *2697–2724.*

This week, identify forms of prayer that could work in your daily schedule. Set aside a consistent time every day to center yourself in God's love and mercy. During this time each day, read and reflect on God's Word. Recollect your heart and offer it to the Lord in your time of prayer.

PART V

JESUS, MY SAVIOR

RECONCILED WITH GOD

BELIEVE

Happiness has been turned into a consumer product. Just walk into a bookstore or search online for books on happiness, and you will find numerous titles offering step-by-step plans for finding happiness and fulfillment in your life. Popular self-help writers invite their readers to discover paths to self-love, self-fulfillment, mindfulness, and personal wellbeing. Like so much else in our society, the search for human happiness has become a million-dollar industry.

Human beings are created for happiness. Yet happiness remains elusive for most of us.

To be a person of faith is to view happiness through the lens of God's plan for the world. It is to recognize that our personal search for happiness will only find its rest when we look above and outside ourselves. Happiness is not to be found in navel-gazing, self-indulgent plans to make "me" the center of existence. We cannot satisfy our own need for happiness. Only God can. And the journey of faith is the exhilarating path of discovering God as the source and end of our life's search for happiness.

To trust in God is to recognize that God *alone* is the source of peace, joy, and happiness. And authentic happiness comes from sharing in that divine source of love and mercy. Riches, honor, fame, and power bring only a fleeting and momentary happiness. This week, as we continue our journey with the *Catechism*, we ask God for greater trust — that he is the source of our deep and lasting happiness. And in doing so, we receive the gift of Jesus, the one sent by God to reconcile us to friendship with God.

Jesus, the Son of God and Savior of the World, is the center of Christian faith. Jesus reveals to us who God is and who we were created to be — children of a loving and merciful God who so desires our friendship that he sent his only Son to suffer, die, and rise again to bring us to new life. In Jesus alone we find the happiness we desire.

WALKING WITH THE *CATECHISM*

"The Word became flesh for us in order to save us by reconciling us with God." *(457)*

In the middle of the Gospel of Matthew, Jesus asks his disciples what we might call a million-dollar question: "Who do you say that I am?" (Mt 16:15). So much of the meaning of life depends on the answer to Jesus' question. Peter's response is the foundation of our faith: "You are the Messiah, the Son of the living God" (Mt 16:16).

Today, that Gospel question is addressed to us. And Jesus offers himself as the answer to the question that is every human life. How do we respond? What meaning does Jesus have for our lives today? This week, take the time to reflect on the *Catechism*'s teaching on who Jesus is and what his life, death, and resurrection mean for our lives.

In *Redeemer of Man*, one of his first writings as pope, Saint John Paul II said:

> Man cannot live without love. He remains a being that is incomprehensible for himself, his life is senseless, if love is not revealed to him, if he does not encounter love, if he does not experience it and make it his own, if he does not participate intimately in it. This … is why Christ the Redeemer "fully reveals man to himself." If we may use the expression, this is the human dimension of the mystery of the Redemption. In this dimension man finds again the greatness, dignity and value that belong to his humanity. In the mystery of the Redemption man becomes newly "expressed" and, in a way, is newly created. He is newly created! … How precious must man be in the eyes of the Creator, if he "gained so great a Redeemer," and if God "gave his only Son" in order that man "should not perish but have eternal life." (10)

This week, take time to reflect on the central mystery of Christian faith, the Incarnation of God in Jesus Christ. Pause to reflect on what the Incarnation tells us about who God is and who we are. Our search for happiness finds perfect fulfillment in God's gift of his Son Jesus — to the world and to each one of us.

MY JOURNAL

Read and reflect on Catechism 456–463.

Spend some time each day this week reading from the Gospel of Matthew. Let Jesus ask you the question: "Who do you say that I am?" Set aside time this week to read and reflect on the *Catechism* sections that describe why the Word became flesh and the meaning of the Incarnation, the heart and sign of Christian faith.

WEEK 18
THE EUCHARIST

CELEBRATE

Jesus, the Son of God, lived as one of us in a particular time and place in human history. But Jesus is not another historical figure of the past, but a real presence in our lives. Jesus desired to be with us always, and he remains present sacramentally in every Eucharist, the repeatable sacrament of initiation. Rooted in the worship of ancient Israel, the structure and prayers of the Eucharist have a rich biblical history. At every Mass Jesus' abiding presence draws us into deeper friendship with God.

Because of this, what we understand and believe about the Eucharist can be life-transforming. For "the Eucharist is 'the source and the summit of the Christian life'" (1324). This teaching of the Second Vatican Council has become a reality for countless generations of ordinary men and women of faith, particularly those who suffer persecution and martyrdom for believing in Jesus Christ.

Take the example of Cardinal François-Xavier Nguyễn Văn Thuận, the Vietnamese archbishop who was imprisoned, tortured, and sentenced to solitary confinement for many years by Communist authorities. He was deprived of food and personal human contact and forbidden to read books or spiritual materials. He found consolation in reciting the psalms and prayers of the Church, which he knew by heart. And every day he celebrated the Eucharist behind bars. If the prison guards had discovered him, he would have been beaten and punished severely. So how did he celebrate Mass in secret?

Cardinal Văn Thuận described his deep love of the Eucharist with moving words: "Every day, with three drops of wine and a drop of water in the palm of my hand, I would celebrate Mass. This was my altar, and this was my cathedral! ... Each day in reciting the words of consecration, I confirmed with all my heart and soul a new pact, an eternal pact between Jesus and me through his blood mixed with mine." With only three drops of wine smuggled into his prison cell, and tiny particles of leftover bread, he was nourished by the Body and Blood of Jesus, who gave him strength to endure violent persecution and hope in his loneliness and desolation.

Few of us will experience the persecutions that Christians face in many parts of the world today. For them, the Eucharist is a source of strength in the face of injustice and violence. Their witness to love of the Eucharist is an example for us to draw on the gift of the Eucharist for our daily journey of faith. If we desire to grow close to God, we should turn to the gift of the Eucharist, in which Jesus draws close to us in the sacrament of his Body and Blood.

WALKING WITH THE *CATECHISM*

"Since Christ was about to take his departure from his visible form, he wanted to give us his sacramental presence. ... In his Eucharistic presence he remains mysteriously in our midst as the one who loved us and gave himself up for us." (1380)

The *Catechism* tells us that the Eucharist is the "source and summit" of the Christian life. The Word of God invites us to make the Eucharist the center of our spiritual life and journey of faith. At the Last Supper, Jesus took bread and wine, prayed a blessing to his heavenly Father, and commanded his disciples to take, eat, and drink of the life-giving spiritual food of his own Body and Blood. Then, Jesus offered his Body and Blood on the cross so that we could be reconciled to friendship with God.

The most fitting response of faith to the gift of Jesus' own flesh and blood is thanksgiving. And that is what the word "Eucharist" means. To partake of Jesus' Body and Blood is to live our lives in "Eucharistic amazement," hearts filled always with thanksgiving for the unconditional mercy and goodness of God. The Holy Spirit invites us today, and every day, to live our lives by humbly giving thanks to God, who so desires our friendship that his Son Jesus gives us his own Body and Blood as our spiritual food and drink. With thanksgiving for the gift and mystery of the Eucharist, take time to reflect on how this sacrament can become "the source and the summit" of your faith in Jesus.

MY JOURNAL
Read and reflect on Catechism *1373–1381.*

Be aware of Jesus' presence in the Eucharist in the scriptures proclaimed, the Eucharistic species of bread and wine, the person of the minister, and the community gathered in prayer. Be intentional about acknowledging Jesus' presence in the tabernacle and on the altar during Sunday Mass. If you are able, spend some time this week in adoration. Take a moment in prayer, before or after Mass, to thank God for the gift of the Eucharist and to entrust yourself to Jesus, truly and fully present in the Blessed Sacrament.

WEEK 19

GRACE

LIVE

We cannot save ourselves. We need the help of God. Grace is the help that God pours into the world without cost or merit. Grace is offered to anyone who calls out to God in faith. Knowing that we are not the source of our salvation, freedom, or peace is the first step on the path of spiritual growth. Relying on the grace of God each day, and in all the day's joys and challenges, is the sure path of perseverance on the journey of faith.

From a young age, Karol Wojtyła, the future Saint John Paul II, learned to rely on the grace of God. In his late teens, Karol experienced firsthand the destruction of his country as Poland endured the inhumanity of the Nazis during World War II. Karol belonged to a local theater group whose members were forced underground as the Nazis occupied their city. One clandestine theater performance was particularly memorable, as the young actors gathered in secret in a dark room lit only by a single candle, with no stage props, and curtains drawn tight to muffle the sound of their voices. In the street below, Nazi soldiers marched while they blasted propaganda over crackling loudspeakers, hoping to instill fear in the hearts and minds of the people.

The young actors continued their recitation of Polish poetry in the conviction that their secret performance was a form of cultural resistance, keeping alive the religious and cultural history of Poland. Amidst the chaos of war, Karol eventually lost his family to illness and old age. How did he survive the destruction of his country and the loss of family?

Karol turned to God for help, every day, over and over again. The grace of God strengthened him to survive those dark days and respond to God's call to the priesthood. He would, in time, be called to serve as bishop of Kraków. Decades later, he was elected to the papacy and took the name John Paul II. As pope, his first words to the world were: "Be not afraid. Open wide the doors for Christ."

Grace transforms life and breaks through the barriers that fear sets up in our hearts. The *Catechism* tells us that grace restores what sin damages in us. Grace is real power. Grace is the merciful, forgiving God who is at work to overcome the effects of human sinfulness. It is an invitation to turn away from the illusion of self-reliance and self-sufficiency by placing ourselves in the hands of a loving and merciful God.

WALKING WITH THE *CATECHISM*
"His grace restores what sin had damaged in us." (1708)

Take this week to pause and reflect on the invitation of divine grace. All of us have ways in which we rely on ourselves and not on God, and it is important to recognize where those tendencies are in our lives. God's word calls us to have trust and confidence in divine mercy, as we cannot save ourselves. The more we recognize this, the more we are able to respond to and live in the truth of God's word.

Where do we find God's grace? The *Catechism* tells us that grace is "the *free and undeserved help* that God gives us to respond to his call to become children of God, adoptive sons, partakers of the divine nature and of eternal life" (1996). God's revealed word, the sacraments of the Church, the mysteries of Jesus' life, death, and resurrection, and the gifts of the Holy Spirit are the means by which God's grace is poured out in the ordinary and extraordinary moments of life. Do we turn to this divine offer of help, or do we prefer to rely on ourselves?

With grace, we participate in the life of God, entering into friendship with our Creator and Redeemer. As the *Catechism* notes, grace "introduces us into the intimacy of Trinitarian life: by Baptism the Christian participates in the grace of Christ, the Head of his Body" (1997). So let us ask him to remove any obstacles of fear or pride in our hearts that may be keeping us from accepting his grace, and thus keeping us from living the full, life-giving friendship with God for which we long.

MY JOURNAL
Read and reflect on Catechism *1996-2005.*

Take a few minutes before bed each night this week to write down a moment when God offered you divine help, or grace — and you responded with a "yes." Think about persons, events, and places that have been a source of grace in your life. Thank God for the graces he has already poured into your heart. Ask for a heart that is open to God's help. Reflect on ways you can become more open to the grace of God's help and strength, even in the midst of your busy day.

WEEK 20

THE WORD OF PRAYER

PRAY

Words dominate our lives. Think of the last time you read the written word. Perhaps it was an online article, a magazine or newspaper, a best selling novel, or your email inbox. The words you are reading at this moment come to you on a published page! Words surround and inundate us. We read for information, knowledge, personal or professional growth, and comprehension. We read as efficient consumers of news updated in real time, making us hurried bystanders along the information superhighway. In the daily human exchange of words, printed or spoken, we are left with little time for reflection and contemplation. More and more, we feel like frazzled passengers caught in the 24/7 rush hour traffic that is human communication today.

Prayer is about words of a different kind. The word of prayer is addressed primarily to God in a divine-human dialogue. And the word of prayer arises in the heart and joins the voice of the Church at prayer. Prayer, even when we use words, is steeped in silence that creates the space for God to speak his word of wisdom, love, and friendship.

This week, reflect on what it means to become a person of prayer. Look to the example of Jesus, who shows us how to pray by the prayers that he offers to his heavenly Father. We learn how to pray by looking at the example and words of Jesus in prayer.

Jesus prays with trust in his heavenly Father. Trust is the fundamental requirement of anyone who seeks to grow in prayer. For prayer is a conversation, an exchange of words, between God and a creature created out of love, for love. Only in faith and trust do we truly begin to pray. All the saints teach us this basic lesson in the words we address to God.

The *Catechism* describes the kinds and forms of Christian prayer. In the rich traditions of Christian prayer that have unfolded over centuries and that continue to thrive in the lives of Christians today, each of us can find one or two forms of prayer that suit our personality, time constraints, and the particular place we find ourselves on our faith journey to God.

The *Catechism* highlights various difficulties common to the life of prayer and many objections to prayer (2726–2737). This is a good place to begin our reflection this week. Once we recognize those difficulties and objections to prayer hidden in our own thought patterns and attitudes to God, we are in a better position to recover or rediscover the gift of prayer that restores us to friendship with God.

WALKING WITH THE *CATECHISM*

"When Jesus prays he is already teaching us how to pray. His prayer to his Father is the theological path (the path of faith, hope, and charity) of our prayer to God. But the Gospel also gives us Jesus' explicit teaching on prayer." (2607)

As a wise teacher of prayer, Jesus meets us where we are and leads us to growth in prayer if we follow his example (cf. 2607). Daily conversion of heart and mind, which is the heart of the Christian life, is only possible through daily prayer. How difficult it is to commit to a time of prayer each day! Jesus shows us the path with small steps we can take to place ourselves in God's presence and learn his way of prayer in silent reflection on the word of God.

Throughout the Gospels we find Jesus in prayer at pivotal moments in his earthly ministry. While Jesus knew well the formal prayers of public worship, his lessons in prayer often center around personal conversations he has with his heavenly Father. When he is tempted in the desert, while he prays for the unity of his disciples, and as he institutes the Eucharist on the eve of his passion and death, Jesus' prayer is a cry of the heart raised to God in supplication, thanksgiving, and worship.

Jesus teaches us how to pray. We are invited into a tremendous union with God when we make the words of Jesus our own words of prayer. The name of Jesus itself is a form of prayer, as his holy name makes present his saving work and mission. An ancient form of constant prayer is the traditional prayer to Jesus, known as the *Jesus Prayer*: "Lord Jesus Christ, Son of God, have mercy on me, a sinner!"

MY JOURNAL

Read and reflect on Catechism *2726–2737.*

Ask the Lord to teach you to pray. Take time this week to learn about the different forms of Christian prayer. Reflect on the kind of prayer that suits you best at this time of life. Pray the *Jesus Prayer* for a set period of time each day this week. Perhaps ten minutes a day or as your schedule permits. Note the spiritual fruit — peace, joy, forgiveness — that you experience by praying the *Jesus Prayer*.

PART VI

CONVERSION

KEEPING SPIRITUAL FOCUS

BELIEVE

"Keep your eyes on the ball!" is a familiar word of advice from coaches in many team sports. Focusing on the task at hand is key to being a team player and helps win games. Losing concentration is a sure recipe for losing points and the game itself.

The same advice is true in the spiritual life. The word of God often reminds us of the need to be focused and single-minded in our search for friendship with God. But we know how difficult it is to keep our focus on our desire for God. The responsibilities and cares of the world often take up time and energy, to the point where we lose sight of spiritual realities. We are trapped easily in the illusion that this visible world, with all its joys and challenges, is the only reality. Life's worries and daily trials distract us. We take our eyes off the goal and end up discouraged, stressed, and anxious.

One of the constant qualities we find in the lives of the saints is that their lives were centered on God. In the midst of hardships, persecutions, and even martyrdom, saintly men and women show us that returning to and keeping our gaze fixed on God is the path to peace, joy, and hope. Returning often to God as the center of my being and keeping my inner thoughts and will focused on him allows me to see my life in the light of his loving plan, a plan that is always filled with divine goodness and mercy.

Continuing our journey with the *Catechism*, let's turn to reflect on the spiritual realities of faith that bring us back into focus. Jesus' call to daily conversion of heart and mind, echoed in the teachings of the *Cate-*

chism, is an invitation to renew our spiritual focus. In prayer and silence, we can recall that this world is not all there is; instead, the world of the spirit is real and life-giving. And faith reminds us that only spiritual realities are eternal and life-transforming.

WALKING WITH THE *CATECHISM*

"[Jesus] invites [sinners] to that conversion without which one cannot enter the kingdom, but shows them in word and deed his Father's boundless mercy for them and the vast 'joy in heaven over one sinner who repents.'"
(545)

The Gospels are filled with story after story of Jesus' encounters with men, women, and children who were invited to daily conversion of life. Some responded in faith and were changed forever. Others turned away, perhaps taking a longer road on the journey to faith in Jesus and to the community of believers. No one was left in a neutral state after an encounter with Jesus. They either turned to gaze on Jesus in faith or turned away in disbelief, indifference, or hostility.

The whole goal of the *Catechism* could be summarized in one word: conversion. On the one hand, conversion requires a sincere, repentant heart. But God does not desire to trample us. Instead, the call to conversion invites us to lift up our eyes and focus on God's loving mercy, which restores us to life in him. Faith is a healing gift that restores us to friendship with God in the community of believers that is the Church.

The *Catechism* describes the path of ongoing conversion of heart and mind with inviting and soul-stirring words: "The human heart is heavy and hardened. God must give man a new heart. Conversion is first of all a work of the grace of God who makes our hearts return to him. ... God gives us the strength to begin anew. ... The human heart is converted by looking upon him whom our sins have pierced" (1432).

Jesus' call to conversion continues to echo in every age of the Church. In fact, Jesus invites each one of us today, every day, to draw closer to him in friendship and a life of self-giving love. This week, pause to hear God's word calling you to conversion of life. Let the light of the Holy Spirit help you begin to see those areas of your life that need God's mercy and forgiveness. Thank God for his grace, which continues to strengthen you to persevere in daily conversion of life.

MY JOURNAL
Read and reflect on Catechism *1427–1433.*

Ask God to show you where he is prompting you to "turn back" in your spiritual journey and start walking with him again. Ask him for the grace of conversion — whether for the first time, or a renewed conversion. Make a note of the areas of life in which you need the grace of God for daily conversion. Perhaps it is a harsh temper, an unkind spirit, or some addiction or burden you have carried with you for years. Bring it to God in prayer and ask Jesus for the grace to turn the inner eye of your heart and mind, letting God be the focus of your life once again!

WEEK 22
Breaking Sinful Habits

Celebrate

The Italian painter Caravaggio is widely considered to be one of the most gifted artists of the seventeenth century. His popularity continues even today as his moving images play on the sharp contrast of warm light and deep shadow to evoke dramatic spiritual themes. The genius painter shaped the work of countless artists who imitated his technique of *chiaroscuro*, whereby light and darkness in a painting become visual metaphors for spiritual illumination.

While his artistic works inspired artists and viewers alike, much of what is known about the personal life of Caravaggio is gleaned from police records! He was known to be a sensitive man with an impatient and violent temper. While painting in Rome, he was involved in a vicious fight that led to murder, for which he was sentenced to death. He fled from Rome to Naples and then on to Malta, eventually seeking pardon from the pope for his offenses. While in Naples, he was involved in another violent clash that resulted in physical harm to himself and others.

Perhaps it is no coincidence that many of Caravaggio's masterpieces depict scenes of conversion from sin and the human search for reconciliation with God and neighbor. He offers us such moving scenes as the conversion of Saint Paul; Jesus' call to Saint Matthew; Saint Peter's denial of Jesus; Peter's crucifixion upside down; Judas' betrayal of Jesus; the raising of Lazarus; and Jesus' call to Peter and Andrew to discipleship. Perhaps Caravaggio's masterpieces were inspired by his deep personal desire to find forgiveness and to be reconciled to God and his community.

There's a Caravaggio in all of us. I don't mean, of course, that we're all supremely talented artists like him. Rather, the point of comparison is that even as we strive to create a masterpiece out of our lives for God, we fall short, often and seriously at times. And we simply cannot pull ourselves back up on our own. On our own, we cannot restore the friendship with God that we have broken. We need the grace of God offered freely and in overflowing abundance in the sacraments of the Church.

The *Catechism* invites us, time and time again, into the mystery of God's forgiving love manifest in the life, death, and resurrection of Jesus, the Son of God. Jesus instituted seven sacraments to continue his work of divine healing and forgiveness, in every age and place. As the *Catechism* teaches, "The sacraments are efficacious signs of grace, instituted by Christ and entrusted to the Church, by which divine life is dispensed to us. The visible rites by which the sacraments are celebrated signify and make present the graces proper to each sacrament. They bear fruit in those who receive them with the required dispositions" (1131).

Continuing our journey of faith with the *Catechism* as guide, we reflect this week on the sacraments of the Church and the real power and graces that flow from them. When Jesus' earthly life ended, he desired to continue his saving, healing work of restoring us to friendship with God. The sacraments are privileged signs of God's desire to heal and strengthen us for the journey of life. They are real sources of divine grace and spiritual power, far beyond any presence or power that human achievement can create.

God does not abandon us to figure out the path of life on our own. God so desires to walk with us on each step of life's journey that he sent his only Son into the world to reconcile us to friendship with him. The sacraments of the Church continue this divine plan of reconciliation in our time and place, making God's mercy and friendship available to you and to me.

WALKING WITH THE *CATECHISM*

"The Lord Jesus Christ, physician of our souls and bodies, who forgave the sins of the paralytic and restored him to bodily health, has willed that his Church continue, in the power of the Holy Spirit, his work of healing and salvation, even among her own members." (1421)

"'Those who approach the Sacrament of Penance obtain pardon from

God's mercy for the offense committed against him, and are, at the same time, reconciled with the Church which they have wounded by their sins and which by charity, by example, and by prayer labors for their conversion." (1422)

In the Gospels, Jesus encounters all kinds of illness. There were those who suffered physical illness and received healing and new life from the hand of Jesus. And there were those whose lives were burdened by spiritual illness from the consequences of life choices. Jesus looked with deep compassion on the alienated, the abandoned, and those chained in patterns of indifference or hostility to God. No one who encountered Jesus remained in a neutral place.

The healing power of Jesus' life, death, and resurrection continues to be offered to us today, in every age of the Church, to the end of time. This is the promise of Jesus as he returns to his Father in heaven. It is a promise that we claim in faith.

The Sacrament of Penance is the sacramental means by which we approach God with our sinfulness, with a heart of penitence and with confident hope in the unconditional, never-ending mercy and forgiveness of God. When the priest says, "I absolve you," the word "I" is the "I" of Christ. For it is Jesus, through the priest as minister of the sacrament, who forgives with healing love and restores us to the community of believers. The Sacrament of Reconciliation is the sure spiritual sign by which Jesus continues, even now, to reconcile us to friendship with God and neighbor.

In the words of the *Catechism,* "'The whole power of the Sacrament of Penance consists in restoring us to God's grace and joining us with him in an intimate friendship.' Reconciliation with God is thus the purpose and effect of this sacrament" (1468).

My Journal
Read and reflect on Catechism *1468–1470.*

Reflect on the need for forgiveness, which is part of the human condition. How do you understand the Sacrament of Reconciliation? What obstacles prevent your participation in this sacrament by which we are reconciled to the loving mercy of God and to our brothers and sisters? This week's theme encourages you to seek God's mercy in confession. If you have never done so, make a concrete plan to include this sacrament as a regular part of your spiritual life.

WEEK 23

PERSEVERANCE

LIVE

Perseverance is difficult. Somehow, even when we desire to reject them, certain sins maintain a grip on us. We can easily become frustrated with ourselves as we seek to overcome our weaknesses and grow closer to God.

Every saint also struggled with sin. Wounded by sin, saintly men and women throughout the ages have wrestled with their faults, moral weaknesses, and repeated failings. The saints grow in holiness in and through their struggles, which is why the Church holds up their lives as extraordinary witnesses to faith. The lives of the saints are powerful reminders that sinners are transformed, by the grace of God, into members of the communion of saints. The first steps on the path of transformation are acknowledging sinfulness and striving, with the grace of God, to grow closer to Jesus Christ every day.

Take Saint Teresa of Ávila, the Carmelite nun who lived in the sixteenth century and was the first woman to be named Doctor of the Church in 1970. In her most well-known spiritual writings, *The Way of Perfection* and *The Interior Castle*, this contemplative mystic described her own spiritual struggles with distraction, indifference to prayer, and sinful habits that made her less charitable, less trusting in God. We can all identify with this saintly woman's failings as we face our own doubts or habits that hurt others and ourselves. For the first twenty years of Teresa's religious life, prayer was a challenge and a constant difficulty. That should be a consolation to all of us who struggle with being faithful to daily prayer.

Saint Teresa of Ávila teaches us perseverance. This saintly woman persisted in prayer and on the path of her spiritual journey of faith. While she persevered in prayer, she experienced the love of Jesus raising her up and freeing her from attachment to sinful thoughts and actions. Jesus' look of love pierced Saint Teresa to the heart, and slowly but surely she grew in the spiritual life as she drew closer to Christ.

As we continue our journey with the *Catechism*, let us take time to reflect on the reality of life as struggle. Whether it is the struggle of sinful patterns that burden life, or the challenge of relationships at home or at work, or distractions and obstacles to prayer, we all face struggles. For many of us today, one area of struggle is attachment to screens — our phones, tablets, and computers.

The *Catechism* gives us the wisdom to recognize that the struggle of life is not only part of the human condition, but also a prerequisite for the holiness and peace we desire so deeply. Time and time again, God offers us his grace to raise us up when we fall and to strengthen us to draw close to him and to our neighbor. This week, take stock of those habits and patterns of behavior that prevent you from experiencing the peace, joy, and freedom that God intends for you, his beloved child. With the *Catechism* as guide, ask God to show you how perseverance in prayer will bear good fruit in your life and in the lives of those you encounter.

WALKING WITH THE *CATECHISM*

"It is not easy for man, wounded by sin, to maintain moral balance. Christ's gift of salvation offers us the grace necessary to persevere in the pursuit of the virtues. Everyone should always ask for this grace of light and strength, frequent the sacraments, cooperate with the Holy Spirit, and follow his calls to love what is good and shun evil." (1811)

The gift of faith is offered to all. Yet our sinfulness prevents us from seeing this gift of faith. Sin blinds us with misperceptions about who God is and who we are in God's eyes. Only with the help of God's grace can we truly see how much God loves us, sustains us, and draws us to himself in friendship and love.

On a human level, we know that perseverance, while difficult in the moment, reaps rich rewards in the long term. Athletes know the positive benefits of perseverance as they strive to achieve personal and team goals. From a young age, children are taught not to give up easily but to keep on striving for goals they set for themselves and wish to achieve in life. Without perseverance we give up easily and become discouraged and lacking in purpose. The same is true of the spiritual life!

The *Catechism* invites us into the grace of God, time and time again. It is a guide for the spiritual life precisely because it takes into account our human weaknesses and directs our heart, mind, and will to the grace of God. The teachings of the *Catechism* are not meant to judge or condemn. Instead, they offer us a lifeline to help us persevere in the spiritual life, in prayer, in our participation in the sacraments of the Church, and in our openness to the transforming power and gift of the Holy Spirit.

MY JOURNAL
Read and reflect on Catechism *1996–2005, 2012–2016.*

Take time this week to recognize patterns of weakness that prevent you from drawing close to God. Be honest with yourself, examining all areas of life and relationships in which you need the help of God's grace. Let go of impatience or anger with yourself and resolve instead to seek and rely on God. Identify concrete ways you will persevere in prayer, including participation in the Church's sacramental life. On each day of this week, ask the Holy Spirit for the grace to persevere in growing in friendship with God.

CHRIST ON THE CROSS

PRAY

Saint Francis of Assisi is one of the most well-known and beloved holy figures of the Church. Born in the central Italian town of Assisi in 1182, as a young man he experienced the attractions of wealth, family prestige, and sensual pleasures. But he was deeply dissatisfied. Even as he enjoyed worldly pleasures and material satisfactions, Francis knew in his heart that there was more to life than the comforts and securities of this world. He searched for God — the God who was searching for him.

At the young age of twenty-four, Saint Francis experienced a dramatic personal conversion. This became not just a turning point in his life, but one of many great turning points in the history of the Church. In a moment of spiritual illumination, the young Francis saw, with astonishing clarity, the truth of his own humanity and his total dependence on God's love and mercy. A similar spiritual illumination is accessible to each one of us, if we are open to it.

Thomas of Celano recounts the dramatic story of Francis's conversion. Led by the Holy Spirit, Francis went into the church of San Damiano to pray. As he entered the church, which was in partial ruins, Francis was drawn to kneel before a large crucifix that was still in the church. There he experienced the presence of God in a strong, undeniable way. And then he heard Christ from the cross addressing him personally: "Francis, go rebuild my house, as you see it is all being destroyed."

At first, Francis thought the Lord wanted him to rebuild the physical church of San Damiano. But as he gazed on the image of Jesus on the cross, he knew that his attempt to physically rebuild the ruined church was only a first step in his conversion. The Lord was asking him to re-build his own life in imitation of Jesus' sacrificial love on the cross, and to renew the Church itself, in imitation of Jesus' poverty, humility, and charity. These hallmarks of Franciscan spirituality began with Francis in prayer before the cross of Jesus. Francis knew his life had to become an imitation of Jesus on the cross.

Prayer is a gaze of love, says the *Catechism* (2558). This approach is different from our usual way of thinking about prayer, mostly in terms of our words and actions. The *Catechism* invites us to see prayer as *being* in the presence of God, as gazing at Christ on the cross, in the power of the Holy Spirit. Our words in prayer and the actions that follow are im-portant. But they are meant to lead us to a contemplative, restful gaze in the Holy Spirit, who opens our eyes to see God who reveals his relentless love and mercy in the sacrifice of Jesus on the cross.

WALKING WITH THE *CATECHISM*

"Once committed to conversion, the heart learns to pray in faith. *Faith is a filial adherence to God beyond what we feel and understand. It is pos-sible because the beloved Son gives us access to the Father. He can ask us to 'seek' and to 'knock,' since he himself is the door and the way." (2609)*

Faith involves the mind, heart, and will. Faith is so much more than feelings or thoughts. The *Catechism* offers us a compelling invitation for our spiritual journey when it speaks of faith as a trusting closeness to God. In other words, faith is growing in friendship with God.

The cross of Jesus is a central symbol of Christian faith. We see cross-es in churches, homes, and faith-based schools. And we wear a cross as an outward expression of our being made a new creation in Jesus Christ through the Sacrament of Baptism. Yet its widespread presence can lead us to forget what the cross means for our lives and for the world. Too easily do we forget that Jesus' suffering and death on the cross reconciles, once and for all, heaven and earth, symbolized in the vertical and hor-izontal beams of the cross. Jesus' cross reconciles us to friendship with God. In the cross of Jesus we are given the most amazing gift of faith!

When we pray, we deepen and grow in faith. We come to recognize ourselves as children of God, loved into existence and sustained and strengthened by divine mercy. We come to see Christ in others to the extent that we gaze, like Saint Francis, on the cross of Jesus. For in gazing on the Lord Jesus, we become the one we gaze on — other Christs in the world.

MY JOURNAL
Read and reflect on Catechism *2665–2669, 2746–2751.*

During this week, set aside some time to reflect on the cross, whether in the silence of a local church or meditating on a crucifix in your home. Stay in contemplation of the cross till you begin to see and hear the love of God spoken to you personally. Let your gaze on the cross of Jesus become a moment when you experience Jesus looking on you with his redemptive love. Ask the Lord to fill you with the liberating graces that flow from his sacrifice of love. Respond to God's invitation to friendship offered in the gift of the cross of Jesus.

PART VII

FORMING THE GOOD HABITS OF A FRIEND OF GOD

The Mind of Christ

Believe

The struggle between the forces of good and evil is as old as the human race. Perhaps that explains the popularity of books and movies like *The Lord of the Rings* and *Star Wars*, which revolve around battles between good and evil forces. The struggle for power is deeply embedded in the human condition. From time to time, we even feel the pull and tug of this struggle within ourselves.

The first chapters of the Bible introduce us to this perennial theme as we read about the fall of Adam and Eve (see Gn 3). They were the first to choose the illusory promise of self-sufficiency, self-driven power, and knowledge apart from God. They chose these false goods and rejected trust in and friendship with God. What God intended for his beloved creatures was a communion of trust, unity, peace, and love. Human beings chose self-love, self-reliance, division, and dominance. Power would no longer be received as a gift and exercised responsibly in the order of love and service; instead, it became a means of domination, efficiency, and control.

The Christian life is a life of power, but it's a different kind of power. For Christians, power is not a vague force lodged in the hidden recesses of the heart or sprawled across the galaxy. Power is not an abstract, impersonal energy unleashed in arbitrary, even whimsical ways or controlled by inner thoughts. The Christian faith reveals and gives access to spiritual power that originates from God and returns to God in thanksgiving and praise. For us creatures, the only power that is real is that which is received as a gift from God. So how is one to receive the gift of this divine power?

The Christian life begins and ends in the power of the Holy Spirit. To grow in friendship with God, we need the inspiration, power, and strength that comes from the Holy Spirit. So, who is the Holy Spirit? And how is the Holy Spirit a source of genuine, life-giving power?

To believe in the Holy Spirit is to profess that the Holy Spirit is one of the three divine persons of the Blessed Trinity. The Holy Spirit is a divine person, not an impersonal, arbitrary force. The Holy Spirit is the love of the Father and the Son poured into the world. And the whole of the Christian life consists in growing in the trust and strength that comes from the power of the Holy Spirit, given to us through the ministry of the Church. The word of God and the sacraments of the Church are the privileged instruments by which the Father and the Son are revealed in the power and love of the Holy Spirit. When we open our life to the power of the Holy Spirit, God dwells in us to strengthen and sanctify us with his eternal love, peace, and joy. And that is real, life-transforming spiritual power.

WALKING WITH THE *CATECHISM*

"Through his grace, the Holy Spirit is the first to awaken faith in us and to communicate to us the new life, which is to 'know the Father and the one whom he has sent, Jesus Christ.'" (684)

The *Catechism* teaches us that the Holy Spirit is one of the three persons of the Holy Trinity, of the same substance with the Father and the Son. The Holy Spirit is at work with the Father and the Son to reconcile the world to friendship with God. The Holy Spirit draws close and dwells within us as we begin the journey of faith at baptism. The gift of the Holy Spirit received at baptism is strengthened in the Sacrament of Confirmation and renewed each time we partake of the Body and Blood of Christ. The Church is the place where we come to receive and know intimately the power and strength of the Holy Spirit in our lives.

Throughout the Scriptures, the Holy Spirit is addressed with various titles, including Paraclete or Advocate, Comforter and Consoler, and Spirit of Truth. Many symbols are also used to signify the presence and activity of the Holy Spirit, including water, anointing with oil, fire, cloud, light, and a dove. And the giving of the Holy Spirit to the Church at Pentecost is described in vivid detail in the opening chapters of the Acts of the Apostles (cf. Acts 2:1–41).

The Holy Spirit perfects our imperfections, making us holy by revealing the divine love and the saving work of Jesus in reconciling us to friendship with God. Faith is a gift of the Holy Spirit by which we respond to God's revealing love and grow in imitation of Jesus.

MY JOURNAL
Read and reflect on Catechism *687–702.*

Ask the Holy Spirit to reveal to you the love of God and the saving work of Jesus in your life. List people, places, and events that have been instruments of the Holy Spirit in your journey of faith. Express your gratitude to the Holy Spirit for sanctifying and empowering your life. Set aside time this week to reflect on the gift(s) of the Holy Spirit you need the most at this time in your life. Pray for the gift of faith to open your life to those gift(s) of the Holy Spirit.

TIME IS SACRED

CELEBRATE

The riches of the Church's liturgical year remind us constantly that time itself is holy. Time is sacred, capable of being infused with the very life of God. We receive the time of our earthly life as a gift from God. But over the course of our lives we often do not experience life as a gift. This is clear even in the ways we speak about time. We say that we "spend time," "waste time," "kill time," "run behind time," "crave down time," "communicate in real time," "try to manage time," and yearn to "travel across time." We even say that "time is precious," "time is money!" When it comes to time, we often feel there's simply not enough of it to complete all the tasks that lie before us. As we live by the clock (or race against the clock) each day, time flies by, often out of our control. Through it all, whether we like it or not, time carries us forward.

The first step to finding balance in the midst of the daily rush of life is recognizing that time is, first and foremost, a gift of God. This means seeing time through the lens of faith, which provides a new and different perspective. If we are merely the stewards — the custodians — of our time on earth, we ought to allow God to sanctify our day with divine grace, power, and peace. In place of stress, fear, and being overwhelmed by the day's rush, we can allow God's grace to shed its radiant light on each day. Looking at time through the eyes of faith can fill our days with peace, hope, and joy. When we make time for God, then God makes us into his living instruments of love and mercy.

With the *Catechism*, we develop a Christ-centered view of time through the Church's liturgical year. The Church's liturgical calendar, with its annual rhythm of feasts and fasts, is a series of invitations in time to experience God's grace in the hours, days, weeks, and months of the year. Jesus' victory over sin and death transfigures every minute of human time so that the kingdom of God enters into our time. Now we can experience time, that necessary dimension of human existence, no longer as a racing, unrelenting succession of minutes, hours, and days, but as the living stage on which God draws close to us in friendship over and over and over again.

Take time this week to ponder with eyes of faith how you approach the time you are given each day. Ask yourself these questions:

- Would I experience time differently if I began each day by entrusting it to God?
- Do I take time, even briefly, during the day to become aware of God's presence in my life?
- Do I feel the Holy Spirit as a trusted companion along the time that makes up my life?

This grace-filled way of experiencing time is captured in the words of the psalmist: "But I trust in you, LORD; I say, 'You are my God.' My destiny is in your hands" (Ps 31:15–16).

WALKING WITH THE *CATECHISM*
"The year is transfigured by the liturgy. It really is a 'year of the Lord's favor.' The economy of salvation is at work within the framework of time." (1168)

God desires to live, move, and dwell in our time. When we realize this — that time is not something we give to God when we have a moment to spare, but really his gift to us — then the pace of life itself changes. We take time to listen to God's word and to partake of the sacramental graces that flow from the paschal mysteries of Jesus' life, death, and resurrection. We attend to the Church's liturgical year, not as a burden on our time, but as an invitation to experience the joy, peace, and hope of sanctified time. We come to know how Jesus' resurrection illuminates even the smallest moments of the day. We move from chronological time (*kronos*) to graced time (*kairos*).

The *Catechism* tells us that God's reconciling love is at work within the framework of time (1168). God is eternal, outside of the constraints and limits of time. Yet the Bible tells the story of God's longing to enter into human history from the very beginning. Over centuries, the people of Israel experienced repeatedly God's saving hand in their common history and their personal time. From Abraham to Moses, to the prophets and kings of Israel, God entered into time and space, transfiguring it with divine forgiveness and reconciling mercy. In Jesus, God enters into human history, making sacred the time that marks the human condition.

God entered time to save us. And we can find God often in those moments of the day when we are rushed, burdened, or overwhelmed by the demands of life. As we try to keep pace with the many activities that fill the minutes and hours of each day, we are challenged to recall that time is sacred, a gift from God, and we have a responsibility to live a balanced life in the time we are given. We recall the words of the wise Gandalf to the young Frodo in a poignant scene from *The Fellowship of the Ring*. In response to Frodo's wish that events had not happened in his time, Gandalf agrees and adds this word of advice: "All we have to decide is what to do with the time that is given to us" (J. R. R. Tolkien, *The Fellowship of the Ring*).

MY JOURNAL
Read and reflect on Catechism *1163–1178.*

This week reflect on how much time is set aside for God in your typical day's routine. For reading Scripture? For the sacraments, if your schedule permits?

Make one resolution to spend a little more time with God (or to commit with greater intention to the time you already set aside for him). As you reflect on the teaching of the *Catechism* on the liturgical year, jot down concrete ways you can partake, consistently and fully, of the sanctification of time in the Church's rhythm of prayer. This week, give up some time you would usually spend on yourself, and take the time instead to pray. Then take time to do a work of charity, be present to your family, or serve someone in need.

WEEK 27
PRACTICING VIRTUE

LIVE

We define personal success in different ways. For some, success lies in the strength of relationships with family and friends. Others measure success by professional careers and personal achievements. And still others see themselves as successful when they actively change the world around them. Whatever our measures, we work hard to succeed and constantly strive to be successful in our relationships and in our daily responsibilities.

In his 2008 book *Outliers: The Story of Success*, Malcolm Gladwell looks for a general rule to explain why some people succeed more than others. Is it nature or nurture? Is it innate talent, genius, favorable opportunities, or hard work? Drawing on a 1993 study, Gladwell found one attribute that all successful people seem to have in common. He called it the "ten-thousand-hour rule." Among the many factors that contribute to the achievements of successful people, they all spend vast amounts of time doing what they eventually become well known for. From the Beatles to Bill Gates, from Mozart to Olympic athletes, those who put in ten thousand hours of hard practice in their fields of achievement seem to rise to the top. In support of his case, Gladwell quotes neurologist Daniel Levitin: "The emerging picture from such studies is that ten thousand hours of practice is required to achieve the level of mastery associated with being a world-class expert — in anything." While some later studies challenge Gladwell's thesis, it remains generally true that we become good at something the more we persevere and give effort and time to it.

What if we applied the "ten-thousand-hour rule" to living the Christian life? Could the repeated practice of virtue over time make us more virtuous? The core truth of human nature highlighted in the study is that practice makes us better at whatever we set out to do. In the same way, could our practice of the virtues help us to turn, again and again, to God for the help of his grace? Our human efforts to practice the virtues do not perfect us. But repeated practice of the virtues opens us gradually to the light and strength of God's grace. And God's grace perfects us over time! Growth in virtue comes from turning to the word of God, celebrating the sacraments of the Church, and choosing to do good, over and over again, ten thousand times and more, till God's grace forms us into saints!

This week, reflect on what it means to become a virtuous person. Christians are realists when it comes to the human condition. We know and humbly acknowledge that we are weak, fallen creatures, tainted by sin yet redeemed by the saving sacrifice of Jesus. At our baptism, God poured out the amazing gift of his new life of grace, which continues to unfold in our lives. Yet God chooses to improve and perfect us with our help. So if we want to grow in virtue, we need to choose and do the good, over and over again. This repeated choosing and doing of the good is what we mean by virtue. As we grow in virtue, we find true success as we become the kind of people who can live in friendship with God. In other words, we become living reflections of Christ in the world. We become saints!

WALKING WITH THE *CATECHISM*

"A virtue is an habitual and firm disposition to do the good. It allows the person not only to perform good acts, but to give the best of himself." *(1803)*

Often, the Christian moral life is viewed as a burdensome list of rules, or as a restriction on our human freedom and flourishing. In fact, experiencing the Christian moral life shows it is truly liberating and deeply fulfilling. It is the measure and path to genuine and eternally rewarding success in life!

When the *Catechism* speaks of the virtues, it offers a different lens on the Christian moral life. Virtue is not a constraint on or denial of our humanity; rather, it is the pull we feel toward the good in our concrete daily actions. This pull grows in us with practice over time. "The virtuous person," says the *Catechism*, "tends toward the good with all his sensory and spiritual powers; he pursues the good and chooses it in concrete actions" (1803). Virtue is the habitual, repeated, "ten-thousand-hours" of choosing and doing what is right, just, prudent, and loving so that we become free to embody the very good we desire and long for.

Take this week to reflect on those good habits that have formed in your life over time. We each have habits that help us to love and serve others, just as we all struggle against habits that prevent us from being a witness to faith, hope, and love. We need "ten-thousand-hours" — more than that, a lifetime — of practicing the good to draw closer to God in friendship, and to become living reflections of Jesus in the world. Our journey of growing in virtue can be our greatest success story of all!

MY JOURNAL
Read and reflect on Catechism *1804–1809 and 1812–1829.*

The *Catechism* describes virtue as the habitual and firm disposition to do the good. As you read and reflect this week, consider: Is the practice of virtue in your life easy? What concrete resolutions can you make to grow in the practice of virtue? As you read about the cardinal and theological virtues in the *Catechism*, identify one virtue you know you need, and resolve to follow one daily practice that will help you grow in this virtue.

WEEK 28

INVITE GOD INTO THE ORDINARY MOMENTS

PRAY

The biblical story of Samuel shows us something about our call to experience God's loving presence in the ordinary, routine moments of daily life (cf. 1 Sm 3:1–10). As he falls asleep, the young Samuel hears the Lord's voice calling him by name. Unprepared for this moment, Samuel thinks mistakenly that Eli, the temple priest, is the one calling to him. Then again, as Samuel begins to fall asleep, he hears the Lord calling him by name, three times. Each time, he thinks Eli has called him. Eventually Eli, a wise and prayerful man himself, understands what is happening to the child. He says to Samuel, "Go to sleep, and if you are called, reply, 'Speak, LORD, for your servant is listening" (1 Sm 3:9).

Eli shows Samuel that prayer is a response to God's voice and presence in the most familiar, ordinary moments of the day. Eli guides Samuel to recognize God's voice and to respond in faith with a listening heart.

Each day the Church invites and teaches us to pray, by opening our hearts to hear God calling us by name. Prayer is a conversation that is meant to deepen our friendship with God. We pray when we offer the responses at Mass, sing psalms, recite memorized prayers, meditate in silence, or simply cry out to heaven with spontaneous words flowing from the heart.

One of the secrets of the kingdom of God, revealed to little children, is the discovery of God's presence and love in the ordinary moments of our day (2660). For a Christian, prayer is not a special activity separated from the routines and tasks of daily life. Christian prayer is the heart of life, from which radiates all the joys and difficulties, the happiness and pain of our daily existence. When we bring moments of prayer into our daily, hyperpaced routines, we bring God's healing love and guiding light into each of the moments of our day.

While speaking to God is a necessary part of Christian prayer, listening to God is even more fundamental. This week the *Catechism* invites us to cultivate a heart of listening so we can hear God call each one of us by name, even in the ordinary events and relationships of our day. The more we take time to listen, the more we will hear God's voice. The invitation and challenge of the Christian life is to form in ourselves a listening heart so, like the child Samuel, we can hear God call us by name and respond in faith.

WALKING WITH THE *CATECHISM*

"Prayer in the events of each day and each moment is one of the secrets of the kingdom revealed to 'little children,' to the servants of Christ, to the poor of the Beatitudes. It is right and good to pray so that the coming of the kingdom of justice and peace may influence the march of history, but it is just as important to bring the help of prayer into humble, everyday situations; all forms of prayer can be the leaven to which the Lord compares the kingdom." (2660)

Prayer and life are not separate compartments. Instead, the *Catechism* invites us to see prayer as the radiating center from which our daily life flows. Over and above our efforts to make time for prayer, we are called to pray in the very events and in each moment of the day. As we practice the presence of God in every moment of our day, we find peace, strength, and wisdom in the face of daily joys and difficulties.

The "Jesus Prayer" is one such spiritual practice with a long history in the Christian traditions of prayer. Drawing on biblical words, the Jesus Prayer invokes the name of Jesus in simple, short repetitions that acknowledge Jesus as the Son of God and the source of mercy. As the *Catechism* tells us, "The urgent request of the blind men [in the Gospel], 'Have mercy on us, Son of David' or 'Jesus, Son of David, have mercy on me!' has been renewed in the traditional prayer to Jesus known as the *Jesus Prayer*: 'Lord Jesus Christ, Son of God, have mercy on me, a sinner!'" (2616).

Our invitation and challenge this week is to reflect on ways we can bring the help of prayer into the humble, everyday situations of life, and discover God's presence there. Making prayer a part of the simple moments of our day opens us up to God's life-transforming grace. As our day is permeated by prayer, every joy and difficulty becomes an invitation to encounter God's peace and love.

MY JOURNAL
Read and reflect on Catechism 2650–2660.

Reflect on ways you can make prayer a part of the events and moments of your daily life. Depending on your current habits of prayer, you might consider adding some prayer time to the start of your workday, at mealtimes, during your daily commute, and at the close of the day. Ask the Holy Spirit to show you where he is inviting you to deepen and increase your prayer life in order to grow in relationship with God.

PART VIII

THE WORD OF GOD

WEEK 29

LISTENING FOR GOD

BELIEVE

How many words have you spoken or written today? We may not count each word we speak or write, but innumerable words surround us from our waking moments to the close of each day. Even the book you hold in your hand is filled with written words! Life unfolds today against the backdrop of the so-called Age of Information. As of this writing, it is estimated that more than four billion people use the internet to exchange information in the form of words, sounds, and images. Whether we like it or not, we spend our days awash in the human exchange of words, in our family life, work, and human relationships. The technological means of global, personal, and social communication have accelerated the pace of communication so that words speed across time and space at a dizzying speed.

In social media terms, we "friend," "follow," "like," or "dislike" the people we communicate with. The nature of social media platforms forces us to reduce human words to snappy messages that rely on abbreviations, acronyms, and short phrases. Since words are the currency of exchange of human thoughts and emotions, the way we use words both reflects and shapes how we relate to one another. The meaning and weight of words often gets lost in this Age of Information, accustomed as we are to fast-paced, instantaneous forms of communication. While the benefits of high-speed communication are many, the human capacity to reflect, to evaluate ideas, and to contemplate principles and applications is losing ground. Reaction rather than reflection rules the day; opinion rather than truth carries the argument.

Faith offers a different perspective. With faith, we can see the power of human words in light of the most powerful word: Jesus, the divine Word-made-Flesh, the heart of Christian revelation and faith. God speaks to humanity through his Son, Jesus, the Word of God, who is God. And, as the *Catechism* tells us, "*Sacred Scripture* is the speech of God," the record of God's loving word to humanity, written under the inspiration of the Holy Spirit (81).

God's word builds up and strengthens us with truth, light, and wisdom. Surrounded as we are by the incessant traffic of words in news, opinions, and social media, we are invited to consider the place of God's word in our daily life. With eyes of faith, we turn to the certainty of God's word for wisdom and light for the journey of life. Reading God's word fixes our gaze on Jesus, who alone fulfills our deepest desires for union with God and neighbor.

WALKING WITH THE CATECHISM

"'Sacred Scripture *is the speech of God as it is put down in writing under the breath of the Holy Spirit.*'" *(81)*

As the story of Jesus' life unfolds in the Gospels, we see key turning points in the ministry of Jesus. One such moment occurs when Jesus stands up in the synagogue on the Sabbath to read the words of the prophet Isaiah (see Lk 4:16–21). In that prophetic passage, Isaiah spoke of the one who is blessed with the Spirit of the Lord to bring good news to the poor, free captives, give sight to the blind, free the oppressed, and proclaim a year of favor from the Lord (see Is 61:1–2). Jesus concludes the reading of this passage with words that must have astonished his listeners: "Today this scripture passage is fulfilled in your hearing" (Lk 4:21).

Jesus is the fulfillment of the law given to the people of Israel. Every word of the Old Testament finds its fulfillment in Jesus' life, death, and resurrection. Jesus, the Word of God, is the fullness of God's promise to free the world and each of us from sin and darkness. With divine mercy, Jesus leads us into the freedom and light of divine love. God's word unites what is divided and heals what is broken and wounded.

The words that daily surround us in the news and social media can be sources of information or misinformation. They can enlighten and bring us peace or distort and disturb our view of persons, events, and the world. In the Information Age, words are tools that either dignify and build up or hurt and tear down persons and communities. From our daily experience we are led to ask: What is the place of the word of God in a world awash in words? And how might the wisdom of God's word shine the light of faith, hope, and love into the daily exchanges that make up the Information Age?

Jesus, the eternal and divine Word-made-Flesh, is the heart of Christian revelation and faith. This week we take time to reflect on the place and priority we give to Jesus, the divine Word, as we are enveloped by the words that make up daily existence. In light of the gift of God's Word to humanity the only fitting human response is faith, praise, and thanksgiving. Giving thanks to God for his divine word is the invitation and challenge of this week.

My Journal

Read and reflect on Catechism *101–119.*

Take a few moments this week to reflect on the place and priority you give to God's word. How much time do you spend each day with Sacred Scripture? How can you make consistent time for reading and reflection on God's word each day? This week, perhaps you might begin with setting aside ten to fifteen minutes a day to read Sacred Scripture. Listen for God's voice speaking in and through his holy word.

WEEK 30
WORSHIP: MY LIFE'S VOCATION

CELEBRATE

To worship is to hold a person or thing in high esteem and awe, to reverence it with a place of priority and honor. It involves bowing down or paying homage to someone or something by bending our heart, mind, and will in respect, admiration, and gratitude.

We worship what we admire, respect, and love, whether they be persons, places, or things. You don't need to consider yourself religious or even spiritual to engage in worship. The act of giving worth to someone or something is a fundamental part of being human. We ascribe worth to persons and things all the time through ordinary gestures and words.

For those of us who worship God and seek to place him above everything else in our lives, it can be all too easy to allow worship to become one isolated action alongside the many other activities that engage and interest us. We set aside time for worship on Sunday, and perhaps even during annual retreats or on pilgrimages. Yet once the Sunday obligation is fulfilled, we check the box and move on to the next activity. Even with the best of intentions, we all eventually fall prey to the hyperactivism that fills our days. Worship becomes just one of the many hurried activities that fill the hectic cycles of each week.

The *Catechism* invites us to reflect on the profound meaning of worship and its transformative place in our lives. In the second part, or pillar, of the *Catechism* ("The Celebration of the Christian Mystery"), we are presented with approaches to worship that can be eye-opening and life-changing. Who, what, and how we worship changes who we become and how we relate to God and the world.

The *Catechism* tells us that worship is primarily a meeting of a child of God with their heavenly Father in Jesus Christ and in the power of the Holy Spirit (1153). This is a radically different approach to worship that sets it apart from all other human activities, making it so much more than a weekly obligation to be fulfilled. Worship is our encounter with the one who created us, who sustains our life, who is the goal of our existence. What follows is that God alone is worthy of our esteem, honor, praise, and thanksgiving. Anyone or anything else takes second place when we understand worship as our encounter or meeting with the Triune God. Worship of God puts first things first!

The *Catechism* goes on to speak of worship as a form of dialogue with God (1153). This is a powerful approach to prayer and worship, because dialogue involves two parties, however unequal they might be. To dialogue with God is to grasp the amazing truth that the worship we give God when we gather as a community of believers is only the beginning. Worship is our openness to what God desires to do in our life every moment and every day. To converse with God is to experience the divine presence and saving work of God in the details of daily life. When we worship God, we make room for God to do his divine, loving work of forming us in the image of his Son, Jesus, in the power of the Holy Spirit.

God is the origin, the chief actor or key player, in the act of worship. To worship, then, is to express a response of humble gratitude for God's loving initiative. In other words, worship is, above all, our response to divine grace.

WALKING WITH THE *CATECHISM*

"A sacramental celebration is a meeting of God's children with their Father, in Christ and the Holy Spirit; this meeting takes the form of a dialogue, through actions and words." (1153)

The sacraments of the Church are offered to us as moments of encounter with God's mercy, healing, and redeeming love. They are divinely instituted, sacred moments when we, creatures prone to sin and weakness, meet our Creator and Redeemer, who is rich in mercy and healing love (see 1131). God desires our friendship and wants to restore us to loving union with him and with our neighbor.

The *Catechism* tells us that a "sacramental celebration is a meeting of God's children with their Father, in Christ and the Holy Spirit; this meeting takes the form of a dialogue, through actions and words" (1153). We are invited to move beyond seeing the sacraments as momentary rituals disconnected from the joys and the challenges of daily life. Rather, the word of God invites us to see the sacraments as the divine answer to the deep hunger of the human heart. In the sacraments, we meet and dialogue with the God who created us in and for love. Here we receive worship as a gift in which prayer — whether communal or personal, vocal or interior — lifts us out of our daily existence into the transcendent and holy presence of God.

The invitation and challenge of this week is to reflect on how we approach the sacraments of the Church. Ask yourself: Do I see the sacraments as obligatory rituals that are irrelevant to daily life, or as sacred moments when I bring my entire self into the holy presence of God who created me, loves me, and sustains me at every moment of life?

My Journal
Read and reflect on Catechism *1069–1083.*

Take time this week to reflect on your understanding of worship. List persons, places, and things you greatly admire, respect, and honor. Reflect on why God is worthy of your praise, honor, and reverence. How does your experience of worship express this praise and honor that is due to God? Is the time you spend in worship of God a dialogue with God? Listen with intention this week to the prayers at Mass so you can make those words your own in your weekly and daily experience of worship and praise of God.

WEEK 31

THE VOICE OF CONSCIENCE

LIVE

Superheroes appeal to our imagination. Whether we're young or old, there's something in all of us that enjoys a good superhero tale, from classical myths to modern movies. Watching a superhero overpower an evil villain is deeply reassuring, even when we know the characters and situations are fictional.

The Bible presents a different kind of superhero. The men and women who take center stage in Sacred Scripture are heroes in the spiritual and moral order. They listen to the voice of conscience as they wrestle with spiritual and moral choices that express what it means to live in friendship with God.

King David is one of those biblical superheroes of the Old Testament. A gifted musician, poet, and songwriter, he is revered as the author of many of the psalms. Chosen to battle the giant Goliath when he was only a young shepherd boy, David became a favorite of King Saul (cf. 1 Sm 17). But in time Saul turned on David, out of jealousy and envy. Saul's distrust soon led him to plot the murder of David (1 Sm 18). Their relationship took a dramatic turn when David was given opportunities to right the wrong Saul had done to him. We are told that David goes in search of Saul, and we imagine that revenge is his motive. (The full story can be read in 1 Samuel 26.)

However, the story moves in a different direction, indicating a deeper biblical truth. David finally finds Saul asleep with his spear in the ground above his head and his bodyguards in a deep slumber. David's companion Abishai urges him to seize the moment: "God has delivered your enemy into your hand today. Let me nail him to the ground with one thrust of the spear" (1 Sm 26:8). In a predictable superhero story, this would be the ideal moment for revenge and the restoration of right order.

Instead, David listens to God who speaks to his inner voice of conscience. This shows that David's conscience has been formed by living in friendship with God. He is able to see right from wrong, and he chooses the way of God. David spares Saul's life, even though it is within his easy grasp to end it.

The story of David's encounter with Saul challenges our usual notions of retaliation, revenge, and payback for wrongdoing. We are invited to move beyond the typical superhero equation of grievance equals retribution. We are called to see our world in the light of God's love, which speaks into the innermost depths of our soul.

David lived in strong awareness of God's great mercy toward him, so he was able to give Saul the same mercy. Rather than taking the throne by murderous revenge, David trusted God's voice speaking to his conscience. He knew God would reward his heroic choice to spare Saul's life. And God did.

Like David, we too are called to form our conscience so that we can hear God speak to us in the innermost sanctuary of our heart. As we continue our journey with the *Catechism* as guide, our lesson and challenge this week is to understand the voice of our innermost conscience formed by our friendship with God.

WALKING WITH THE *CATECHISM*

"Deep within his conscience man discovers a law which he has not laid upon himself but which he must obey. Its voice, ever calling him to love and to do what is good and to avoid evil, sounds in his heart at the right moment. ... His conscience is man's most secret core and his sanctuary. There he is alone with God whose voice echoes in his depths." (1776)

No one escapes the inner voice of conscience. It remains an essential part of human experience, even if we ignore it or are distracted by other voices around us. Saint John Henry Newman reasoned for the existence of God from the human experience of conscience. He argued that the experience of conscience was evidence of God's existence, for where else does this inner voice come from if not from a transcendent being. If we hear that convincing, inner voice telling us to do good and avoid evil, there must be a divine, transcendent being who is speaking to and through the innermost sanctuary of the human heart.

The *Catechism* tells us that we discover deep within us a law which is not of human origin, but which we must obey. This inner voice echoing in the depths of our hearts can be heard particularly when we face a choice between right and wrong, good and evil. We are inclined to choose and do the good through this inner prompting of conscience.

However, there are other perspectives that view conscience as a burden that limits our freedom and prevents us from achieving full human fulfillment. In this view, conscience must be overthrown in favor of license, or the sheer will to do what I want to do, apart from and against any authority, human or divine, over my life. Instead of following the law our Creator has written on our hearts, many today seek autonomous self-expression shaped and guided only in reference to personal feelings, desires, and needs.

The *Catechism* presents a different picture to be considered with the eyes of faith. We are invited to see that conscience, first and foremost, calls us to love as God loves and to see the choices before us with God's vision. God creates everything out of and for love. For baptized Christians, the voice of conscience echoing deep in our heart is the presence of the Holy Spirit, the third divine Person of the Blessed Trinity who dwells in us. Conscience guarantees that those who live in friendship with God are free to choose good and avoid evil, a freedom that God desires for us.

This week reflect on your experience of conscience. Think about the ordinary moments of your day — at home, at work, or at school — when you are faced with small or great choices. Reflect on those concrete, daily opportunities to listen to God's voice speaking to the innermost sanctuary of your heart and mind. These are moments to let God speak to you and guide you on the way of love that transforms even a simple child into a spiritual superhero!

MY JOURNAL
Read and reflect on Catechism *1776–1794.*

This week, jot down personal instances of listening to the inner
voice of conscience. In light of the *Catechism*'s teaching on conscience, reflect on how your experience of conscience reveals the
presence and activity of the Holy Spirit in your life. List concrete
ways you continue to form your conscience in light of God's word
and the teachings of the Church. Maybe your formation takes
place through daily reading of God's word and participation in the
Church's sacramental life, particularly the Eucharist and confession. Perhaps you form your conscience through ongoing spiritual
reading or listening to a favorite podcast. Identify and commit to
a practical plan to make a daily examination of conscience during
which you express gratitude to God for each day and pray for the
grace to overcome weakness and sin.

WEEK 32

Praying with Scripture: The Lord's Prayer

Pray

"Screen time" is a familiar phrase used to describe the minutes or hours we spend looking at some form of digital screen, whether it be a computer, tablet, or mobile phone. Studies point to a growing number of children and teenagers who are considered to be addicted to electronic screens. Chris Anderson, father of five and former editor of *Wired*, describes the addictive nature of screen time in a rather stark way: "On a scale between candy and crack cocaine, it's closer to crack cocaine."

Members of the iGeneration who have grown up using iPads, iPhones, and various forms of social media are accustomed to communicating through screens. Poll after poll confirms that the iGeneration spends countless hours of "screen time" streaming and surfing the web and social media, or playing games on smartphones, computers, or televisions. This dependence on screens, however, is not limited to children and youth. More and more adults spend excessive time in front of screens, becoming as addicted to screen time as children and youth. The social distancing imposed in light of the global pandemic of 2020 drove us more often and closer to our screens, whether we liked it or not.

"What if we turned to our Bible as often as we do our smartphones?" said Pope Francis to pilgrims gathered in Saint Peter's Square one Sunday afternoon (March 5, 2017). "What would happen were we to treat the Bible as we treat our mobile phone?; were we to always carry it with us, or at least a small, pocket-sized Gospel, what would happen?; were we to turn back when we forget it ... were we to open it several times a day; were we to read God's messages contained in the Bible, as we read telephone messages, what would happen?"

Pope Francis's question is intriguing. It is an invitation to anyone struggling with or helping others in the struggle against excessive dependence on screen communication.

We are created with the capacity to communicate with God and others through our words, our actions, and the decisions that guide our lives. Created as social beings, we desire to communicate from a young age. We come into this world learning to communicate within our families, and we grow and flourish in human communication as we journey through life within various communities.

The word of God is the speech of God, God's communication with humanity. With eyes of faith, we receive with gratitude God's word as a powerful and revelatory divine communication. From the first to the last pages of Scripture, God and humanity are engaged in a breathtaking dialogue. God speaks a divine, creative word of love, and humanity responds in thanksgiving, blessing, petition, intercession, and praise. This divine-human conversation is captured in the refrain that marks the forming of a covenant between God and the people of Israel: "You shall be my people, and I will be your God" (Jer 30:22).

This week, as we continue our journey with the *Catechism* as guide, we turn our focus to the Bible as a teacher of prayer, with particular attention to the Lord's Prayer. We discover that prayer is the communal and personal participation in the divine-human communication that overflows from the pages of Scripture into the concrete reality of our lives. If you desire to learn to pray, the great figures of the Bible are wonderful role models of prayer. From Genesis to Revelation, we see biblical figures in deep, ongoing, and personal dialogue with God. Noah, Abraham, Moses, and Isaiah address God as creator of the universe, as helper in times of distress, and as a friend worthy of praise and thanksgiving. In the Gospels, we find Jesus deep in prayer before important moments in his earthly ministry. And Jesus teaches his disciples, and us, how to pray when he gives us his own words of prayer in the Our Father, considered the "summary of the whole Gospel," the "most perfect of prayers," and the "center of the Scriptures" (2774). And Mary, mother of Jesus and mother of the Church, is revealed in the Gospels as the teacher of prayer *par excellence*!

WALKING WITH THE CATECHISM

"'The Lord's Prayer is truly the summary of the whole gospel,' the 'most perfect of prayers.' It is at the center of the Scriptures." (2774)

If I desire to grow in the spiritual life, prayer is essential. Yet I know well the many obstacles and stumbling blocks to a fruitful, consistent practice of prayer: The hectic pace of daily life, the multiple distractions and worries that race into and grip the mind as one begins to pray, or the dryness or emptiness when one turns to God.

The Bible is a treasured source of prayers. On almost every page of Scripture we encounter models of prayer who address God as a confidant, helper, advocate, and friend. The whole of Scripture could be seen as the graced unfolding of an ongoing conversation, a continuing dialogue between God and humanity. Nowhere else do we see more clearly that God desires our friendship and offers, time and time again, his covenant of love to bind us to him as his beloved children and friends. For this reason "the Church ... specially exhorts all the Christian faithful ... to learn 'the surpassing knowledge of Jesus Christ' (*Phil* 3:8) by frequent reading of the divine Scriptures. ... [P]rayer should accompany the reading of Sacred Scripture, so that a dialogue takes place between God and man". (2653).

The *Catechism* notes that "in Sacred Scripture, the Church constantly finds her nourishment and her strength, for she welcomes it not as a human word, 'but as what it really is, the word of God.' 'In the sacred books, the Father who is in heaven comes lovingly to meet his children, and talks with them'" (104). We are reminded that "the Christian faith is not a 'religion of the book.' Christianity is a religion of the 'Word' of God, a word which is 'not a written and mute word, but the Word which is incarnate and living.' ... Christ, the eternal Word of the living God, must, through the Holy Spirit, 'open [our] minds to understand the Scriptures'" (108).

One prayer among the many found in Scripture stands out as a perfect guide to Christian prayer: the Our Father or Lord's Prayer. Because many of us learned this prayer at a young age, its riches can be overlooked easily because the words are so familiar. In the Lord's Prayer we are given not only a prayer that Jesus taught his disciples (and us), but one that Jesus prayed himself. When we pray the Lord's Prayer, we say the same words that Jesus spoke to his heavenly Father! We enter into the loving conversation between the Father and the Son on our journey of friendship with God.

This week we pause to consider how we can enter into the enduring conversation between God and humanity, as described in the pages of the Bible, through the Lord's Prayer. The sure path to taking our place at the table of the divine-human dialogue is to draw close to the rich meaning of each word of this prayer. When I turn to God's word as a teacher of prayer, I become an active participant in the conversation that God desires to have with his friends. By remaining close to God's word, I learn how to address God as a friend, following the example of many biblical figures whose lives were transformed by their encounter with God. Praying the Our Father with renewed understanding, we become better conversation partners with God, who looks on us with unconditional love as his son or daughter, and as a friend.

Praying with the Bible throughout the day can also be an excellent antidote to excessive screen time!

MY JOURNAL
Read and reflect on Catechism *2650–2660, 2759–2776.*

This week's general focus of reflection is praying with the Scriptures, with particular focus on the Our Father. From your reading of the *Catechism*'s sections you will learn how the word of God can become a trusted anchor and companion that enriches daily prayer. Then reflect on the *Catechism*'s summary of the origin and the central place of the Our Father in the liturgical celebrations, prayers, and devotions of the Church. Choose one article of the Lord's Prayer and reflect in depth on the *Catechism*'s explanation of the meaning of the selected article (2777–2856). Pray the Lord's Prayer slowly and mindfully each day of this week. Reflect on how you've drawn closer to scripture as a companion in prayer.

PART IX

FRIENDSHIP WITH GOD'S PEOPLE

WEEK 33

BE WHO YOU ARE: THE BODY OF CHRIST

BELIEVE

The desire to live a long, healthy life is universal. People from all regions and cultures of the world search for secrets to longevity. In a 2015 best-selling book titled *The Blue Zones Solution*, author Dan Buettner describes the lifestyles and daily habits of people around the world who live the longest, healthiest lives, living into their eighties, nineties, and even beyond.

Among the "secrets" of those who live to a ripe old age is a strong sense of belonging to a faith-based community, family, and social circle. People who live long lives tend to do so within close-knit families, faith communities, and social networks that nurture and strengthen spiritual and emotional needs. Today, many people say they consider themselves spiritual but not religious. Instead of seeking out institutionally framed faith communities, they look to nurture their spiritual life on their own. What are the long-term impacts of this kind of isolation? Is it essential to faith to become part of a community of believers, however flawed that community may be, in the past or in the present?

As we continue our journey with the *Catechism* as guide, we turn this week to consider the social and communal nature of the act of faith. We live in an age that emphasizes the private act of faith. And yes, faith is always profoundly personal — it is my free response to the loving initiative of God who desires my friendship. Yet the invitation to faith is also, of necessity, an invitation to community. God's call is extended always to a people, a community who together learn to love God and neighbor, however imperfect and flawed the journey might be.

The *Catechism* invites us to see that the same "secret" to human happiness found in bonds of family and community is also true of the spiritual life. Faith in God necessarily opens us to the community of believers called into friendship with God. As human beings, we find belonging, growth, and happiness within an intricate web of human connections and relationships. The same is true of the spiritual life. We cannot believe, says the *Catechism*, without being carried by the faith of others, in the present and in the past (166). Faith connects us to a community of believers not only in our own time and place, but in every time and place through centuries of the Church's existence and life. A person of Christian faith is never alone!

The paradox of faith in Jesus Christ is that it is both intensely personal and communal at the same time. In the Gospels, when Jesus called individuals to follow him, their response of faith immediately placed them within a community of believers who supported and sustained faith. When we partake of the Body and Blood of Jesus in the Eucharist, we become what we receive, as Saint Augustine once noted (1396). The sacraments unite us to Christ, who unites us to all those who make up the Body of Christ, the Church.

To profess faith in Jesus Christ means that we are never alone. We belong to Christ's Body, the Church, which he instituted as his ongoing presence in the world. This Church is at once holy and always in need of purification. The Church is holy because it originates from the wounded side of Jesus on the cross, and it is always in need of renewal because it is made up of sinners, like me.

WALKING WITH THE *CATECHISM*

"Faith is a personal act — the free response of the human person to the initiative of God who reveals himself. But faith is not an isolated act. No one can believe alone, just as no one can live alone. ... I cannot believe without being carried by the faith of others, and by my faith I help support others in the faith." (166)

Can I be a person of faith in isolation? Our natural human experience reveals a truth of the spiritual life: we need strong bonds of human relationships and community to nurture and support us in faith. We place our trust not in the human beings who make up the community of believers, but in Jesus, the founder and head of his Body, the Church.

From the beginning of his public ministry, Jesus invited his disciples into a community of faith. And Jesus spoke of the intimate union that exists between him and his disciples. As he instituted the gift of the Eucharist, Jesus proclaimed a mysterious union between his own body and ours when he said, "Whoever eats my flesh and drinks my blood remains in me and I in him" (Jn 6:56).

To put one's faith in Jesus and to live in the power of God's word draws one into the Body of Christ, the Church. In this body, Jesus' own life is communicated and shared by those who believe. By partaking of the sacraments, we are united in a real way to Jesus in his passion, death, and resurrection. The unity of faith and the diversity of the members of the Church go hand in hand. The act of faith incorporates each believer into the family of the Church that Christ established as the visible sign of his ongoing presence in the world. Throughout history, this visible and invisible community has remained the source of life-giving faith, finding its origin and holiness in Jesus.

My Journal
Read and reflect on Catechism *166–169, 781–801.*

Set aside time this week to reflect on the place of the community of believers, the Church, in your spiritual life. Identify challenges and obstacles you or someone you know may face in living in this community. List every person who has helped you in one way or another on your spiritual journey. Trace your spiritual family tree, noting each person whose witness has supported and strengthened your faith. Give thanks to God each day of this week for one person who has nurtured your faith in Jesus Christ. Invite someone you know to experience the local parish and faith community that has nourished your faith. Sometimes it just takes a simple and warm invitation for someone to move from being spiritual to being religious!

WEEK 34

LITURGY: UNITING HEAVEN AND EARTH

CELEBRATE

Some years ago, we happened to attend Sunday Mass at Holy Cross Abbey, a Trappist monastery nestled in the stunning Shenandoah Valley of the Virginia countryside. It was a perfect spring day, and the deep silence, characteristic of monastic places, was interrupted only by spontaneous sounds from the natural world. Birds in full-throated song, cattle mooing while grazing in the surrounding fields, and insects buzzing in alertness to springtime were part of nature's symphony unfolding outside as Mass began in the austere, yet exquisite, monastery church.

An older woman with her granddaughter sat in the pew in front of us. The young girl was close to our son's age at that time, about seven. It seemed obvious that this was the first time the little girl had seen monks at prayer. Her innocent eyes were wide open in amazement as the white-robed men processed into the choir stalls, chanting the prayers and hymns of Mass. The young child was not distracted in the silent beauty of this sacred place. Instead, her childlike gaze was riveted on the monks as they praised God in word and sacrament.

After Mass ended, the woman turned to her granddaughter as they prepared to leave the church. We couldn't help overhear her whispering to the child, "So what do you think of this church?" The little girl paused for a moment, looked around the church, and then replied innocently, "Grandma, in this church it feels like we're in heaven!" Our son looked at us and nodded in silent agreement.

In her simple response, that little girl captured what we hold in faith: the earthly liturgy is a participation in the heavenly liturgy. The Eucharist unites heaven and earth!

The *Catechism*'s description of the nature and the purpose of Christian liturgy contains some of the most beautiful passages of this spiritual guide. We are not left to come up with our best plans as we reach out to God. If we desire friendship with God, the liturgy is the sacred event in which this divine-human communication grows and flourishes. Every liturgy not only recalls Jesus' suffering, death, and resurrection, but also celebrates and opens us to the saving power contained in those sacred events. Our desire for God is met by God's desire for us. In every liturgical celebration we are lifted up into the life-giving company of Jesus in his sacramental presence. The liturgy is an earthly celebration of our divine origin and our final destiny in God's presence. By our participation in the earthly liturgy, we are practicing for heaven!

WALKING WITH THE *CATECHISM*

"In the earthly liturgy we share in the foretaste of that heavenly liturgy ... toward which we journey as pilgrims, where Christ is sitting at the right hand of God." (1090)

"Christian liturgy not only recalls the events that saved us but actualizes them, makes them present. The Paschal mystery of Christ is celebrated, not repeated. It is the celebrations that are repeated, and in each celebration there is an outpouring of the Holy Spirit that makes the unique mystery present." (1104)

What are concrete ways to grow in friendship with God? Through our journey with the *Catechism*, we have considered paths to deepen faith. Daily reading of Sacred Scripture, particularly the psalms, and time set aside for personal prayer and reflection are just some of the ways to draw close to God. Each person's spiritual journey is unique; the goal is to grow in friendship with God.

When we participate in the liturgy of the Church, the focus shifts from our efforts to what God is doing in us and for us. In the cycle of liturgical feasts and fasts, the deeds of God in the past are made sacramentally present in our time, in every time. In the sacraments of the Church, we are taken up into what God does for creation, which is nothing less than restoring the cosmos and each individual to friendship with God. At every Eucharist, the priest and the people at prayer together look at the Lord Jesus in the mystery of his saving death on the cross and are sacramentally incorporated into his new, resurrected life. We celebrate the liturgy as our humble, grateful response of worship and thanksgiving for all of God's mighty deeds for and among us.

We do not bear the burden of spiritual growth on our own. This realization is truly liberating. Recall that we reflected at the beginning of this journey with the *Catechism* that faith is, first and foremost, a response to God's loving initiative. The free gift of divine grace is at the origin of our being and daily existence. In the Eucharist, something is happening that no one, not even the saintliest person, could make happen: God is continuing his healing and merciful work of reconciling his people to friendship with him!

My Journal
Read and reflect on Catechism *1076–1109.*

Reflect on what participation in the Eucharist means for your spiritual life. When you are at Mass this week, take time to read the words of the readings and prayers, and reflect on them. We pray the words of Mass but rarely take time to ponder the meaning of the words we say each Sunday. Jot down one Mass response that you will reflect on this week in light of the *Catechism*'s teaching that the earthly liturgy is a participation in the heavenly liturgy. Pray for the people around you during the Mass, both the familiar faces and strangers. Reach out to someone you would like to invite to Mass, perhaps a Catholic who has fallen away from the Church or someone who is interested in the Catholic faith.

THE PARISH COMMUNITY: A LIVING CATECHESIS

LIVE

"I can't believe this is actually happening?" This was the deep-felt sentiment, spoken and unspoken, on the minds and hearts of many as the COVID-19 virus began to spread rapidly around the world, bringing normal daily life to a shuddering halt in 2020. The most gifted novelists and creative movie makers could not have imagined the unfolding scene as the coronavirus unleashed devastating physical, economic, and social effects on the world. As the disease spread, it left in its trail an unprecedented amount of fear, uncertainty, hardship, suffering, and death.

Even as the deadly virus spread, witnesses to the strength and resilience of the human spirit, now under severe test, began to manifest far and wide. As cities went into lockdown and social distancing became the norm of human interaction, the kindness and compassion that lies hidden within us surfaced. Families, friends, and neighbors came together with concern for the elderly and vulnerable, and communities recognized the need for self-sacrifice for the sake of the common good.

The experience of a global pandemic will not be forgotten easily. The shared experience is a stark reminder of the vulnerability of the human condition. The opening chapters of Genesis introduce us to this perennial theme as Adam and Eve fell from God's friendship. Since then, powerlessness is a necessary part of human existence. God intended a communion of trust, peace, and love with the creatures created out of love. Human beings chose self-love, division, and dominance. Community was no longer received as gift and nurtured in love and service, but became a means of division and control.

It often takes crisis moments, such as the global pandemic that broke out in 2020, for people to recall a fundamental truth of the human condition: we exist in and for community. We are essentially social beings, meant to live our unique individuality within interwoven circles of communities in family, church, neighborhood, society, and the world. From beginning to end, life unfolds in successive communities in which faith, hope, and love flourish.

Community is a fundamental truth of faith and of human existence. The natural bonds of community we experience every day parallel the supernatural bonds that exist in the inner life of God and the Church. God is a community of divine persons whose love overflows into the world, which is created, redeemed, and sanctified by the Holy Trinity. We profess this truth of Christian faith each Sunday, as we pray together the Creed affirming that our God is an eternally loving unity of divine persons, a community of Father, Son, and Holy Spirit.

Each Christian is baptized in the name of the Father and of the Son and of the Holy Spirit. What does this mean? For one, it means that faith as a disciple of Jesus begins, rests, and ends in the community of the Holy Trinity. When we are baptized in the name of the Trinity of divine persons, we receive God's merciful invitation to friendship with the Father through the Son in the power of the Holy Spirit. Just as we cannot live without human communities, we grow each day in the spiritual life in loving communion with the Triune God and the community of the Church.

The *Catechism* tells us that "a parish is a definite community of the Christian faithful established on a stable basis within a particular [local] church," or diocese (2179). The parish is not only a setting for receiving and nurturing faith, it *is* the living Body of Christ in our midst. Through our visible parish community, we participate in the divine life promised to the universal Church. In our parish, the love of God continues to be present in word and sacrament and in our community's works of charity.

Baptism calls us to nothing less than a share in the life and love of the Blessed Trinity. We can accept that divine invitation by participating more fully in the sacramental life and service of our parish community.

WALKING WITH THE *CATECHISM*

"A parish is a definite community of the Christian faithful established on a stable basis within a particular church. ... It is the place where all the faithful can be gathered together for the Sunday celebration of the Eucharist. The parish initiates the Christian people into the ordinary expression of the liturgical life: it gathers them together in this celebration; it teaches Christ's saving doctrine; it practices the charity of the Lord in good works and brotherly love." (2179)

Saint John Chrysostom, prolific early Christian writer and bishop, wrote, "You cannot pray at home as at church, where there is a great multitude, where exclamations are cried out to God as from one great heart, and where there is something more: the union of minds, the accord of souls, the bond of charity, the prayers of the priests" (2179).

During the global pandemic of 2020, many people were forced into social isolation and separation from the sacraments. Strangely enough, many people grew in their appreciation for their parish community through the experience of being deprived of the communal celebrations of the sacraments. Even with the practice of "spiritual communion," there was a deep-felt void in the absence of the community assembled to hear God's word and respond in worship and thanksgiving.

Granted, personal communion with God is very much part of the tradition of Christian prayer. Our personal prayer, however, should lead us to desire the prayer of the community assembled at prayer. For the Church is the visible community in which we enter into the life-giving presence of the Triune God, who is a community of divine persons.

The *Catechism* reminds us that the Eucharist stands at the center of a parish community. Gathered around the table of the Lord with the priest who leads the community at prayer, we are caught up in the communion of the Blessed Trinity and the unity of the Body of Christ. All parish activities, programs, and initiatives flow from the central gift of the Eucharist, where God calls and unites his people into a living community of faith to set the world ablaze with the fire of his love.

My Journal
Read and reflect on Catechism *2177–2188.*

This week in your journal, note your experiences and recollections of belonging to a parish community. List both positive and negative experiences as you reflect on the *Catechism's* teaching. If you belong to a parish, renew your commitment to participating in the Eucharist each Sunday, and as often during the week as your time permits. As you reflect on the importance of belonging to a community of faith, consider how you might give of your time, treasure, and talents to your parish, even if you begin with a small commitment. You might consider writing a thank you note to your pastor or a parishioner whose dedicated commitment contributes to the life of the parish. If you do not belong to a parish community, consider visiting a nearby parish or reaching out to a parishioner to inquire about the sacramental life and spiritual activities of the parish.

THE PRAYER OF THE CHURCH

PRAY

Can you imagine a three-hour-long movie with no narrated commentary, artificial light, or added sound effects, and only a few minutes of spoken words? That movie is *Into Great Silence*, a masterful documentary by German filmmaker Philip Gröning. Released in 2005, this unique film portrays the life of Carthusian monks as they go about their daily routine in the Grand Chartreuse, a remote monastery in the French Alps.

When Gröning approached the monks with his request to film their life, he was told the community would consider his request. The monks responded to the filmmaker with an invitation to shoot the movie ... sixteen years later! Gröning came by himself, with no camera crew, to live in the monastery of the Grand Chartreuse. There, he entered into the grand silence of monastic life for six months over the course of two years. He filmed and recorded on his own with no artificial light or sound effects. The result is a uniquely absorbing film that invites the viewer into a hidden and silent life that is like no other.

The monks of the Grand Chartreuse belong to an ancient religious community called the Carthusian Order, founded by Saint Bruno in 1084. Like all religious vocations, the life of a Carthusian monk or nun is a response to a divine call. In the case of Carthusians, men and women answer God's call to live an austere immersion in solitude and silence centered on the continual praise of God and growth in union with Jesus Christ in his word and sacrament. Each day, the words spoken by a Carthusian monk or nun are addressed primarily to God in prayer, in chanting of hymns, and in personal prayer and study of Sacred Scripture. The center of a monk's life is God, approached and contemplated in total, fruitful silence. At the heart of the monastic rhythm is the prayer of the Eucharist and the praying of the psalms.

Few of us are called to live the life of a Carthusian monk! But every Christian is called to a life of prayer. The Church offers each one of us the psalms as an essential and permanent element of prayer rooted in the word of God. The psalms are master classes in prayer. As we continue our journey with the *Catechism* as guide, we are invited this week to discover how to let the psalms become an essential part of our daily prayer and growth in the spiritual life.

The psalms express the whole range of human emotions as the psalmist, standing in the presence of God, communicates with God from the depths of his heart, mind, and soul. If we desire to learn how to pray as a disciple of Jesus, the psalmist is a master teacher who leads us on the path of conversation with God. Joy, thanksgiving, patient hope, anger, disappointment, and even despair are just some of the emotions that the psalmist pours out to God in prayer. Think of the many emotions you have felt today, and you can be sure to find a psalm or two that reflects and expresses those emotions in the presence of God.

We live out our life's vocation immersed in the worlds of home, work, and community, with all their noise, stress, distractions, and pressures. We may not be able to pray all 150 psalms in one week, as Carthusian monks and nuns do, but, we can set aside time in the midst of the activities of each day to join in the prayer of the psalmist, who lifts up his eyes and voice to God in praise, thanksgiving, pleading, intercession, and petition. By praying the psalms, we enter into the silence of our hearts and minds, even if only for a few hurried minutes each day, to bathe in the radiant presence of God who desires nothing less than our friendship and love.

WALKING WITH THE *CATECHISM*

"The Psalter is the book in which The Word of God becomes man's prayer. ... [T]he same Spirit inspires both God's work and man's response. Christ will unite the two. In him, the psalms continue to teach us how to pray." (2587)

Praying the psalms in the Liturgy of the Hours is one way to grow in daily prayer that feeds the spiritual life. Within the Liturgy of the Hours (also called the Divine Office), the Church prays the psalms throughout the day, from Morning Prayer through Night Prayer and all the hours in between, making the entire day holy by offering it in praise to God. The Liturgy of the Hours, as a part of the "public prayer of the Church" (1174), allows the faithful to pray constantly, transforming ordinary moments of each day with God's grace and presence.

Praying the psalms throughout the day is one way to sanctify time and bring our attention back to God in the midst of the noise and busyness of life. Just as all the baptized are called to holiness and Christian witness, all the faithful are invited to join in this prayer of the Church, rooted in the psalms. As the *Catechism* notes, "Prayed and fulfilled in Christ, the Psalms are an essential and permanent element of the prayer of the Church" (2597).

Every human emotion finds expression in the prayerful words of the 150 psalms. The psalmist, writing hymns under the inspiration of the Holy Spirit, is familiar with the real-life conditions that frame the human desire to communicate with God. So, when we take up the psalms, we are learning at the feet of a spiritual guide. The psalmist is a wise spiritual companion leading us closer to God through our thoughts and emotions lifted to God in heartfelt prayer.

"The Psalter is the book in which the Word of God becomes man's prayer," says the *Catechism* (2587). All the books of the Old Testament recount God's work in creating the world and establishing a covenant of love with the people of Israel. The psalms, sung to God, highlight God's saving actions in history and our human response of faith and love to God's goodness. Jesus unites God's saving work and the human response of faith in his life, death, and resurrection.

At every Mass we pray one psalm in the responsorial psalm, sung between the Scripture readings. Each responsorial psalm is chosen carefully to convey the human response to God's word proclaimed in the readings of the day. Another long-standing tradition of Christian prayer introducing us to the psalms is the Liturgy of the Hours or Divine Office. This practice of prayer draws deeply from the wellspring of the 150 psalms so that the hours of each day are made holy by the praise of God. Prayed in the mystery of God revealed in Jesus Christ in the power of the Holy Spirit, the Liturgy of the Hours is a practical and steady way to bring one's joys and worries into God's presence and to enter into the divine-human communication in the ordinary moments of our day.

The psalmist's words are sustained constantly by the praise of God. This week consider how you will make the psalms prayed in the Liturgy of the Hours part of your daily prayer. Reflect on the spiritual desires and longings echoed in the psalms: "simplicity and spontaneity of prayer; the desire for God himself through and with all that is good in his creation; the distraught situation of the believer who, in his preferential love for the Lord, is exposed to a host of enemies and temptations, but who waits upon what the faithful God will do, in the certitude of his love and in submission to his will" (2589).

Pick up one of the psalms today and pray the words of the psalmist slowly. Let the psalmist's words of praise, thanksgiving, and petition fill your heart and mind with peace, joy, and hope. Let the simple prayer of the psalms bring the presence of God into your busy day.

MY JOURNAL
Read and reflect on Catechism *1174–1178.*

Take time this week to become familiar with the Liturgy of the Hours or Divine Office. There are several print and digital resources to help you, such as Magnificat, Divine Office, Laudate, eBrieviary .com, and iBreviary. All of these serve as easy-to-use introductions to this tradition of prayer. Learn the various parts of the Liturgy of the Hours, such as Morning Prayer, Evening Prayer, and Night Prayer. Make a plan to pray the Liturgy of the Hours at least once a week, either with others or in personal prayer. You might consider joining with others in your parish or faith community who pray the Liturgy of the Hours. Is God calling you to begin a parish group devoted to praying the Liturgy of the Hours together?

PART X

THE CHURCH

WEEK 37

THE CHURCH: HUMAN AND DIVINE

BELIEVE

St. Peter's Basilica in Rome is the iconic heart of the universal Catholic Church. The monumental basilica frames many news photos of popes greeting crowds of pilgrims. What is not as well-known to the public are the elaborate excavations deep beneath this historic church that are the center of worldwide Catholicism.

Some forty feet below St. Peter's Basilica lies an ancient Roman city that dates back almost two thousand years to the time of the Roman emperors. Excavations begun in the 1940s, during the papacy of Pius XII, sought to locate the resting place of Saint Peter, believed for centuries to be buried beneath the present-day basilica. The excavations unearthed a second-century city with an elaborate network of narrow streets, passageways, and catacombs, where wall markings point to the remains of several early Christian individuals and families.

From early Christian times, it was believed that the Apostle Peter was martyred sometime between AD 64 and 67, during the reign of the Emperor Nero in the adjacent Circus of Nero. The Christians of Rome carefully buried the apostle's remains and built a shrine in his honor a century later. He was revered as the first Bishop of Rome, to whom Jesus gave leadership of the universal Church. In the fourth century, the Emperor Constantine decided to build the first church of Saint Peter, known as Old St. Peter's Basilica. Centuries later, from 1506 to 1626, construction of the present basilica replaced the original Constantinian church with a masterpiece of Renaissance architecture from the creative genius of Bramante, Michelangelo, Maderno, and Bernini.

When excavators in the 1940s discovered human bones in a marble lined opening in a graffiti wall covered with inscriptions, they were convinced that they had found the relics of Saint Peter. Today, the highlight of the tour of the excavations reveals that a plumb line from the top of Michelangelo's magnificent sixteenth-century dome falls directly above the location where the bones of Saint Peter rested. In this sacred church, the words of Jesus to Peter are almost literally true, "And so I say to you, you are Peter, and upon this rock I will build my church" (Mt 16:18).

The Catholic Church makes the unique claim that the Church is both visible and spiritual, a hierarchical society and the Mystical Body of Christ. These two components of the Church are inseparable. One cannot understand the Church without reference to both elements at the same time. And this is why the Church is a mystery, accepted with the eyes of faith.

In recent decades, scandals and divisions have focused attention on the all too human side of the Church's life and witness. This human aspect of the Church is as old as the Church herself, journeying through history in periods of decline, division, and even disgrace. The *Catechism* reminds us that the Church is undividedly human and divine (771), originating in the blood and water that flowed from the side of Jesus on the cross (766). The Church exists as a sacramental reality, whose deepest reality goes beyond any human institution, however significant in mission and achievement.

The Catholic Church is the only institution on earth to profess it is both human and divine. Our faith invites us into the mystery of this human-divine institution as the sacrament of our salvation and the means by which we are reconciled to friendship with God.

WALKING WITH THE *CATECHISM*

"The Church is both visible and spiritual, a hierarchical society and the Mystical Body of Christ. She is one, yet formed of two components, human and divine. That is her mystery, which only faith can accept." (779)

In recent decades, the scandalous revelation of multiple cases of abuse in the Church — both in this country and around the world — has shaken the faith of many. And as the weaknesses and failures of the human, visible side of the institutional Church are revealed, the nature of the Church itself comes into focus. What is the origin and nature of the Catholic Church? How will the Church endure in its mission and witness when it is so plagued by scandal and deep division?

The *Catechism* tells us that the Church is born from the community of divine persons that is the Blessed Trinity of Father, Son, and Holy Spirit (758). Yet the Church is also made up of human beings, weak and tempted by every form of sin. The *Catechism* summarizes it this way: The Church is a plan born in the Father's heart, prepared for in the Old Covenant, instituted by Jesus Christ, and revealed by the Holy Spirit (759–768). Jesus established and sustains *his* Church as a visible organization through which he communicates truth and grace to all men. The visible, human component of the Church is subordinate to the spiritual reality of the Church. This is a significant truth of faith.

The origin of the Church is divine, not human, and this divine source alone is the guarantee that our faith in Jesus Christ is not in vain. We place our trust in the divine origin of the Church in the midst of the most divisive and scandalous moments in her history. In every age, God renews the Church in the mystery of his Son's death and resurrection, and the unifying, life-giving power of the Holy Spirit. Encountering the human component of the Church is an invitation, time and time again, to place our trust in the divine component of the Church. Let us pray for eyes of faith to see and live in the mystery of the Church that is at once visible and spiritual, scarred by sin and radiant in divine beauty.

My Journal

Read and reflect on Catechism *758–771.*

Reflect on the words of Matthew 16:18, when Jesus entrusts his Church to the Apostle Peter. Peter's own life was marked by moments of deep faith and profound betrayal. From your reading of the *Catechism*, list three responses you would offer to someone whose faith in the Church has been shaken by scandals and divisions. Take time in prayer to identify any aspects or teachings of the Church that you find difficult to understand or uncomfortable to accept. Bring these to God in prayer.

WEEK 38

THE SACRAMENTS: GOD'S MASTERWORKS

CELEBRATE

Few will argue that the majestic frescoes of the Sistine Chapel changed the path of Western art. Commissioned by Pope Julius II and completed by the Renaissance genius, Michelangelo, between 1508 and 1512, the private chapel has been used by popes since the sixteenth century for papal liturgies and as the iconic setting in which a new pope is elected in a conclave.

The Sistine Chapel is awe-inspiring in scale, beauty, and design. The lowest part of the ceiling depicts various Old Testament figures who prefigured Christ, such as Abraham, David, and Jonah, and the prophets of Israel like Isaiah, Jeremiah, Ezekiel, and Daniel. Then in the highest part of the vault, Michelangelo depicts his unforgettable vision of the creation of the world, Adam and Eve in the garden of Eden, and the Great Flood with Noah and his ark. All in all, Michelangelo brings to life some three hundred biblical figures, from Genesis to the final coming of Christ at the Last Judgment. The sacred space measures some 134 feet long and 44 feet wide, providing over 5,000 square feet of fresco art.

Artistic and architectural works like the Sistine Chapel remind us of higher, spiritual realities. Perhaps this is why Saint John Paul II referred to the frescoes of Michelangelo as a "pre-sacrament." Beauty, in artistic forms, predisposes and opens us to God. Beauty prepares the heart and mind to receive the graces that flow from the Church's sacramental life.

The *Catechism* describes the sacraments of the Church as "'powers that come forth' from the Body of Christ" (1116). The sacraments are "masterworks of God," who so desires our friendship that he continues to pour out his divine love in the graces that flow from each of the sacraments (1116). These special avenues of grace, healing, and friendship with God have great spiritual power for our daily lives. If we desire to grow in union with God and the community of believers, the sacraments are the means that God continues his saving, healing, and reconciling work in the world.

Just as we appreciate masterpieces of art, we are invited to consider the spiritual masterpieces of the sacraments, through which we enter into the very life and love of God and love of neighbor. No beauty or power created by human genius compares with the beauty and power of the sacraments, by which the Holy Spirit continues to act in the Church so that you and I may be made into a spiritual masterpiece for God.

WALKING WITH THE *CATECHISM*

"Sacraments are 'powers that come forth' from the Body of Christ, which is ever-living and life-giving. They are actions of the Holy Spirit at work in his Body, the Church. They are 'the masterworks of God' in the new and everlasting covenant." (1116)

This week we turn to reflect, with the *Catechism* in hand, on the meaning of the sacraments and their place in the spiritual life. God meets our deepest spiritual longings with sacramental signs taken from the natural world — water, wine, bread, oil, light — that he infuses with radiant divine life, healing, and strength. The sacraments confirm, time and time again, that God does not abandon his creation and the creatures he brings into existence, but journeys with us every step of the way.

The *Catechism* defines and describes the nature and effects of the seven sacraments of the Catholic Church: Baptism, Confirmation, Eucharist, Penance, Anointing of the Sick, Holy Orders, and Marriage. The teachings of the *Catechism* on the sacraments are contained in Part II, titled "The Celebration of the Christian Mystery." The sacraments are not burdensome and repetitive rituals: They are celebrations of God's awesome, healing presence by those who gather in faith, hope, and love. Each sacrament corresponds to the way we were created by God as embodied spirits.

"The sacraments are efficacious signs of grace, instituted by Christ and entrusted to the Church, by which divine life is dispensed to us" (1131). While each sacrament effects unique graces in the life of a Christian, they all share common elements. All seven sacraments are instituted by Jesus Christ to continue his saving work accomplished during his earthly life.

The purpose of all seven sacraments is to nourish, strengthen, and express faith by building up the Church and worshipping God. The seven sacraments "confer the grace that they signify," that is "they are *efficacious* because in them Christ himself is at work" (1127). The *Catechism* speaks of "sacramental grace" as the grace or divine help of the Holy Spirit, given by Jesus and proper to each of the seven sacraments (1129). Both on a personal and communal level, the seven sacraments invite us into a new life of grace with God in Christ Jesus in the power of the Holy Spirit. What a great mystery of faith it is to live a sacramental life!

MY JOURNAL
Read and reflect on Catechism *1113–1134.*

Reflect on what these sacraments mean to your spiritual life: baptism, confirmation, and the Eucharist. Have you received some or all of these sacraments? Do you continue to participate in the Church's sacramental life, particularly the Eucharist and confession? If not, list the reasons why. If yes, list spiritual fruits you have experienced over time from this participation. Make one spiritual resolution this week to help you enter more deeply or return to the sacraments. Ask the Holy Spirit to show you how to help someone you know to experience the power and the beauty of the "masterworks of God."

WEEK 39

MORALITY AS A RESPONSE
OF LOVE

LIVE

How often we hear it said that Christianity is a religion of burdensome, harsh rules that no one could possibly live by. The moral demands of the Christian life are seen as unrealistic ideals that set an impossible standard of life that few can live up to. God is perceived as a severe taskmaster who expects humanity to live by unrelenting and ultimately unachievable demands. Christianity and its way of life are swept aside as unattainable and therefore irrelevant.

This is where the saints of the Church come in. For they turn this way of thinking about Christianity upside down. The saints are God's masterpieces. They demonstrate by the witness of their lives that the moral demands of Christianity can be lived by — and that the pursuit is eminently worthwhile. More importantly, the saints' lives are proof that the moral demands of Christianity can *only* be lived up to with grace and the spiritual strength that comes from God. This is the courageous, even daring, adventure embodied in the life of every saint.

Take Saint Maximilian Kolbe, a spiritual hero of the twentieth century, who gave his life to save another in the dreaded Nazi concentration camp of Auschwitz during World War II. The story of his martyrdom is a powerful reminder of the primacy of love and grace that stands at the heart of the commandments of Scripture and the moral teachings of the Christian life. Kolbe's life, like the lives of countless other Christian saints, points to our most fundamental responsibility for the well-being and good of one another.

Born in the late nineteenth century, Kolbe became a Franciscan friar at a young age and excelled as a student of philosophy and theology. Ordained a priest in 1918, he set about encouraging devotion to Mary, the Blessed Mother of God, under the title of her Immaculate Conception. Soon after the Nazis occupied Poland in 1939, Father Kolbe began to assist Jewish refugees who were fleeing persecution and extermination. In early February 1941, the monastery in which Father Kolbe lived was shut down, and he was arrested by the German Gestapo and imprisoned. A few months later he was transferred to the concentration camp at Auschwitz.

When one of the prisoners at Auschwitz escaped, the Nazi prison commander chose ten men to face death by starvation, as a warning to other prisoners. One of the men, Franciszek Gajowniczek, pleaded with the prison guard to spare his life, as he would never see his wife and children again. Hearing his anguished plea, Father Kolbe stepped forward and offered to take his place. He did not know the man, but God's grace strengthened him to offer the ultimate sacrifice of his life for a person in need.

Father Kolbe remained calm and prayerful in the last days of his life, after two weeks of dehydration and starvation. He died by lethal injection on August 14, 1941, one of too many innocent lives lost in the horror of the Nazi Holocaust. Saint John Paul II canonized Saint Maximilian Kolbe on October 10, 1982, declaring him a "martyr of charity."

Saint Maximilian Kolbe, like so many saints and martyrs of the Church, is living proof that the Christian moral life is not a set of unrealizable, burdensome rules designed to diminish our freedom and deprive us of human dignity. To live the Christian life is to grow in freedom to choose the path of selfless, self-giving love that desires only the good of the other. For love is willing the good of the other, as Saint Thomas Aquinas teaches.

God is the source of love who strengthens us to love in a way that goes beyond our limited and weak human capacity. To love as God loves is the heart of the Christian moral life, which originates in love of God and flows out into love of neighbor. When we choose to live by God's commands, we become a living channel and willing instrument of divine love in the world.

The moral life is never easy, but it leads to genuine freedom as it conforms us to God and confirms our inestimable worth and dignity as his children. When God's love begins to inspire our words, actions, and thoughts, we become a living reflection of Jesus in the world. This is the less traveled path of the greatest spiritual adventure, well known to the saints. For saintly men and women show with their lives that it is not only possible to live the demands of love, but to rise to the heights of moral heroism with God's grace and help. The saints demonstrate that one can freely and joyfully choose to live even the most demanding moral teachings of Christianity.

WALKING WITH THE *CATECHISM*
"The precepts of the Church are set in the context of a moral life bound to and nourished by liturgical life. ... [They are] meant to guarantee to the faithful the very necessary minimum in the spirit of prayer and moral effort, in the growth of love of God and neighbor." (2041)

"I like to contemplate the holiness present in the patience of God's people: in those parents who raise their children with immense love, in those men and women who work hard to support their families, in the sick, in elderly religious who never lose their smile. In their daily perseverance I see the holiness of the Church militant. Very often it is a holiness found in our next-door neighbors, those who, living in our midst, reflect God's presence. We might call them "the middle class of holiness." (*Gaudete et Exsultate*, 7)

With these words, Pope Francis invites us to attend to the witness of the "saints next door," who are able to live by God's command of love because they rely on God's grace. This is why the saints make good spiritual companions on the journey of life.

It is possible to live a good, even heroic, moral life. We ourselves make small and big acts of heroism in our daily lives: spouses for one another, parents for children, children for parents, and neighbors and friends caring for one another in times of distress.

Instead of approaching the Christian moral life in fear and anxiety, or doubt and indifference, the *Catechism* invites us to recognize that love, divine and human, is the core of every one of the moral teachings of the Church. When we allow God's self-giving love to be the motivation and the inspiration of our actions, words, and deeds, we already travel the path of the Christian moral life. Reflect on your own moral strengths and potential as you take time this week to read and reflect on the five Precepts of the Church, described in the *Catechism*, paragraphs 2041–2043.

The *Catechism* speaks of the moral life as "spiritual worship" (2031). Do we consider our daily moral actions and decisions to be worship of God? Do we experience moral decisions as anxious burdens or mere expressions of self and acts of self-determination? Faith offers a different perspective that liberates from the burden of sin and preserves our human dignity, in both the short and long run. The Christian moral life is an invitation to experience the great adventure of becoming a saint!

MY JOURNAL

Read and reflect on Catechism *2030–2031, 2041–2043.*

Take time to reflect on your approach to moral decisions, and to the commandments and the precepts of the Church. Jot down positive as well as negative thoughts and feelings you may have about the demands of the Christian moral life. Bring any obstacles and doubts to God in prayer, asking for the grace to experience the love that inspires and strengthens moral decisions. Read a short account of the life of a saint you have always wanted to know more about or a saint you look to as an example of Christian living. Write down reasons why this saint speaks to your life and how the moral heroism of the saint's example helps you overcome fear and encourages you on the path of Christian living.

Ask, Seek, Knock as a Friend of God

Pray

In the classic cartoon *Calvin and Hobbes*, the mischievous Calvin is known for pushing the envelope with his parents. In a typical exchange, Calvin approaches his mother with a series of persistent requests in the hope of wearing her down. He starts off with two clearly inappropriate requests: "Mom, can I set fire to my bed mattress? Can I ride my tricycle on the roof?" To these outlandish requests, his mother simply says, "No, Calvin." Finally, he zeros in on to what he hoped for all along: "Then can I have a cookie?" Once again, his request is denied, at which point Calvin gives up and says with a sigh, "She's on to me."

If you are a parent, grandparent, or teacher, you know how persistent a child can be when requesting a favorite toy, food, or article of clothing. Children can be determined, even obstinate, when making requests or bargaining with those in authority over them. The persistence behind a child's request can wear down even the most resolute of adults.

In the Gospel, Jesus points to the simple human gesture of parents giving good gifts to their children to illustrate the nature of prayer (cf. Lk 11:11–13). Jesus compares God's gracious gift of the Holy Spirit to the generosity of parents who desire to give their children only good gifts. In Genesis, God and Abraham engage in a remarkable conversation as Abraham bargains with God in the hope that divine mercy will prevail, and the innocent will not be punished along with the guilty (Gn 18:23). And in the psalms David pleads with God persistently for justice against the wrongdoings of his enemies.

God is generous beyond our imagining. Prayer is our conversation with God when we place ourselves in his presence and discover the immense ocean of his merciful love for us. God's limitless generosity is the foundation of our faith and hope whenever we turn to him in prayer. And yet it seems that we do not always receive the precise answers or specific outcomes we ask for. Being in conversation with God makes us the better for it. Persisting in prayer draws us closer to seeing the ways of God that are often beyond our understanding.

This week we set aside time to reflect on Jesus' invitation to approach God by asking, seeking, and knocking in the words and thoughts that form our prayers (cf. Lk 11:9). What are the things we most desire from God? Perhaps they are temporary needs, or requests that have long-term, eternal consequences. God knows what is in the depths of your heart, spoken or unspoken. Coming into the presence of God, in the Eucharist or in personal and family prayer, we are invited to take on the attitude of heart and mind that delights God — an attitude of faith, humility, and gratitude. Then, as we "ask," "seek," and "knock," whether our prayers are answered or not, we are in a win-win situation as we find a peace that surpasses all understanding and draw closer to God in friendship.

WALKING WITH THE CATECHISM

"Once committed to conversion, the heart learns to pray in faith. Faith is a filial adherence to God beyond what we feel and understand. It is possible because the beloved Son gives us access to the Father. He can ask us to 'seek' and to 'knock,' since he himself is the door and the way." (2609)

Our attitudes of mind and heart are as important as our words and commitment to times for prayer. When Jesus invites us to "ask," to "seek," and to "knock," he shines a light on the inner dispositions, feelings, and thoughts that make prayer effective. We are challenged to go beyond measuring the effectiveness of our prayers only in terms of requests heard or petitions answered. We begin to look at prayer through the wider lens of our filial relationship and friendship with God, not as a bartering tool or a zero-sum game.

God does not need our prayers. We need prayer to deepen our faith and to strengthen our trust and confident hope in God. Prayer binds us closer to God in friendship.

Persistence in prayer can be a challenge. We may wonder why we need to place our petitions before God over and over again. Doesn't God hear our prayers the first time we express them? Why does it seem that our prayers are not heard? What is the point of "asking," "seeking," and "knocking" if answers to prayer are slow to come or remain elusive after many years?

The *Catechism* treats prayer in realistic terms when it speaks of the "battle of prayer" (2726). Perhaps that is what prayer feels like on most days — a battle against time and our many interior and exterior distractions. Yet we are given strong encouragement to draw from the wisdom of the *Catechism* in its teaching on prayer. We are reminded that "[p]rayer is both a gift of grace and a determined response on our part. It always presupposes effort. ... We pray as we live, because we live as we pray. ... The 'spiritual battle' of the Christian's new life is inseparable from the battle of prayer" (2725).

Given the hectic pace of daily life, we often experience prayer on the periphery of our rushed existence. We squeeze in times of prayer whenever we have a moment to pause before the word of God, pray the Liturgy of the Hours, or participate in the Eucharist. When times of prayer become fruitless or a drudgery, the *Catechism* brings us back to the joyful and hopeful heart of Christian prayer. The fourth part of the *Catechism* offers rich guidance on the nature, forms, and ways of Christian prayer. When our feelings don't move or inspire us to pray, we can heed the *Catechism*'s reminder that in prayer, "Christ comes to meet every human being. It is he who first seeks us and asks us for a drink. Jesus thirsts; his asking arises from the depths of God's desire for us. Whether we realize it or not, prayer is the encounter of God's thirst with ours. God thirsts that we may thirst for him" (2560).

MY JOURNAL
Read and reflect on Catechism *2725–2745.*

Take an inventory of your prayer life. When and how often do you pray? What challenges do you experience in praying with the word of God and the Church's prayer of the Liturgy of the Hours? Does your personal prayer flow from and prepare you for the prayer of the Eucharist, the source and summit of all Christian prayer? What attitudes of mind and heart are you called to develop so that prayer becomes a wellspring source of peace, hope, and joy each day? Jot down the difficulties you encounter as you make time for prayer. Reflect on one idea or teaching of the *Catechism* on prayer that helps you overcome your obstacles to pray.

PART XI

MARY: A MOTHER'S GUIDE TO FRIENDSHIP WITH GOD

WEEK 41
MOTHER OF GOD AND MOTHER OF THE CHURCH

BELIEVE

In the web of human relationships that make up daily life, we remember the circumstances of first meetings with those who eventually become good friends or even our spouse! When longtime friends or couples talk about how they first met, they often recall the person who introduced them or the setting in which they first introduced themselves to each other. A friend introduces a friend who in turn introduces a friend and the ever-expanding circle of human friendships ripples into families, neighborhoods, and communities.

Among the many people who can introduce us to friendship with God, there is one special figure who merits attention as we continue our spiritual journey — Mary, the mother of Jesus, who God set apart for a unique role in salvation history. God chose Mary to bear his only Son, Jesus, in his Incarnation among us. Jesus loved his mother with surpassing divine love and filial tenderness. And the Holy Spirit overshadowed Mary so that her "yes" to the Archangel Gabriel at the Annunciation would bear the divine fruit of Jesus, the only Son of God, who came into the world. From the moment of her conception, Mary was "full of grace" because God preserved her from the stain of original sin. Only a pure, sinless creature could carry in her body, mind, and heart the immensity and intensity of God's grace as the Mother of God.

So what better person to introduce us to friendship with God than the mother of Jesus, God's only divine Son! What better person to point to and lead us closer to Jesus than his own mother, Mary, the spouse of the Holy Spirit! What better way to come to know the love of God than through the love of Mary for her Son Jesus and the love of a divine Son for his Blessed Mother!

Over centuries, Mary is the female name that has been pronounced most often in the Western world. Without doubt, Mary has been portrayed in art and music more than any other woman in world history. The person and life of the Blessed Virgin Mary is the subject of many of the world's most treasured works of art. It's safe to say that the Mother of God has inspired more people than any other woman in the history of Christianity. So why is Mary, the mother of Jesus, so important in the history and spiritual life of Christians?

In the Creed prayed each Sunday, we profess belief that Christ "was conceived by the power of the Holy Spirit and born of the Virgin Mary." In reflecting on these words of the Creed, the *Catechism* follows the life of Mary from her miraculous Immaculate Conception and birth, to the Annunciation, and through her divine motherhood in God's plan of salvation. After Jesus' earthly life was over and he fulfilled perfectly God's plan by his suffering, death, and resurrection, his mother Mary continued her maternal role in the order of grace.

As the one who heard God's word and responded in faith, Mary is the first and most perfect disciple of Christ. So as you continue your spiritual journey with the *Catechism* as guide, look to Mary as your spiritual mother. Mary desires nothing less than to be your mother in faith! The Mother of God is the woman God chose for the singular role of bearing Jesus, his Son, into our fallen world. For this reason, the Church has always invited the faithful to turn to Mary as our mother in faith. For just as we enter the world with the help of a mother, we grow in the Christian life with the help of a spiritual mother. The Blessed Virgin Mary is our spiritual mother, whose unique and singular role is to always lead us closer to her Son Jesus so we might grow in love and friendship with God.

WALKING WITH THE *CATECHISM*

"Jesus is Mary's only Son, but her spiritual motherhood extends to all men whom indeed he came to save." (501)

"What the Catholic faith believes about Mary is based on what it believes about Christ, and what it teaches about Mary illumines in turn its faith in Christ" (487). These words from the *Catechism* summarize the way to approach Mary as our spiritual mother — that is, our mother in faith. The *Catechism* tells us that Christians give Mary a special place in the spiritual life because her "yes" to God was a pivotal, first step in the unfolding of God's loving plan to reconcile us to friendship with him. Mary's "yes" to God reversed the "no" of Adam and Eve, allowing every creature to begin anew the journey of being restored to friendship with God (488).

In Mary, the Word became flesh and entered the human condition. Mary journeys with her divine Son, Jesus, through every stage of his earthly life, from his birth and public ministry to his betrayal and suffering, his death on the cross, and his glorious resurrection. No other human being was physically and spiritually closer to Jesus than his mother was. Shouldn't we want to draw close to Mary, if we desire to be close to her Son, Jesus? By turning to Mary as our mother in faith, she introduces us and becomes a guide like none other, leading us closer to the mystery of her Son's Incarnation, life, death, and resurrection by which we are saved.

What a mystery of faith her life and her role in salvation history is. No wonder artists and musicians have painted, sculptured, and sung Mary's praises for the past two thousand years!

My Journal

Read and reflect on Catechism *484–511 and 963–975.*

The *Catechism* describes the vocation, life, and spiritual role of the Mother of God in great depth. Read and reflect on the paragraphs listed above as a way to let Mary introduce herself to you. Then let Mary introduce you to her divine Son, Jesus, as you learn about Mary's role in salvation history and in the spiritual life of every Christian. Let Mary lead you to friendship with Jesus in her roles as the Mother of God, the Mother of the Church, and our Mother in Faith.

Take time this week to reflect on your understanding of Mary and her place in your spiritual life. Jot down questions, doubts, or misgivings you have about devotion to Mary. Identify talents and gifts, like faith, courage, or hard work, you have received from those who play a maternal role in your life — your mother, grandmother, an aunt, or other significant maternal figures. No matter what your relationship with Mary is now, ask Mary to be a mother accompanying you on your spiritual journey. During times of prayer this week, seek her help and intercession for you and your loved ones.

WEEK 42

MARY: WOMAN OF THE EUCHARIST

CELEBRATE

Walk into any Catholic Church in the world, and there's a good chance you'll see an image of the Blessed Virgin Mary in sculpture, stained glass, mosaic, fresco, or paint. Some of the most exquisite hymns ever written sing the praises of Mary's life and role in God's plan of salvation, most notably the *Ave Maria*, composed and arranged by Schubert, Bach, and Gounod. Throughout the liturgical year the Church celebrates Marian feast days, including those dedicated to her Immaculate Conception and birth, the Annunciation, her Assumption and crowning as Queen of Heaven, and her role as Mother of God and Mother of the Church. The celebration of the Christian mystery in the Church's sacramental life and liturgical calendar has always included celebration of the person and life of Mary, Mother of God.

Devotion to Mary has been part of the Catholic sacramental tradition from the very beginning of the Church's existence. As early as the third century, the first Christians, who celebrated the Eucharist in the hidden underground catacombs of Rome, painted on the catacombs' walls a fresco image of Mary and the Child Jesus seated on her lap. Since the event of the Annunciation, recorded in the opening chapters of Luke's Gospel, there has never been a time in our Church's history that Mary has not been a focus of spiritual reflection, study, and celebration.

Why has Mary inspired so much liturgical celebration and artistic beauty over the centuries? Can devotion to Mary be explained away as pious and prescientific naiveté? Or is there something in the unique maternal figure of the Mother of God that answers a profound spiritual longing of the human heart? The Church's celebration of Mary points to the mysteries of the Incarnation, life, death, and resurrection of her divine Son, Jesus. The person and life of Mary of Nazareth, as recounted in the Gospels, invite us to unite ourselves to her as spiritual children as we celebrate the saving mystery of her Son.

This week we continue reflection on the figure of Mary, who invites us to let our lives be transformed by the celebration of the mystery of her Son. It is worth noting, as a reminder, that Catholics do not worship or idolize Mary, as is sometimes claimed by critics. Rather, we revere and honor Mary because of her unique place in God's plan to restore humanity to friendship with him. Because of the singular role Mary was given to be the Mother of the Son of God, Catholics look to Mary in spiritual need and in veneration. We do not give to Mary the worship that is due to God alone.

Mary's entire life pointed to her Son, Jesus. And in every celebration of the Christian mystery, Mary stands ready to lead us to Jesus. So the Church rightly points to Mary as our teacher in contemplating, as she uniquely did, the face of Jesus. As the *Catechism* notes, "All the signs in the liturgical celebrations are related to Christ: as are sacred images of the holy Mother of God and of the saints as well. They truly signify Christ, who is glorified in them" (1161).

Mary accompanied Jesus in every historical event of his Incarnation, from his birth and childhood, through his earthly ministry, to his death and resurrection. And just as she is a mother to her divine Son, Mary desires to be a spiritual mother and to accompany anyone who journeys through life as her Son's disciple. The Church looks to and celebrates Mary as the one who "shows the way," leading us always beyond herself to Jesus, who even now reconciles us to friendship with God (2674).

WALKING WITH THE *CATECHISM*
"In celebrating this annual cycle of the mysteries of Christ, Holy Church honors the Blessed Mary, Mother of God, with a special love." (1172)

The world was in turmoil in 1531. Countries were ravaged by earthquakes and wars. Entire nations and peoples were being torn away from the unity of the Church as the Reformation spread across the lands of

Europe. After Christopher Columbus's attempt to find a western sea route to Asia that ended in the discovery of the New World in 1492, an extended period of European colonization of the Americas began to unfold in the early sixteenth century. It was in this tumultuous historical setting that the Mother of God, under the title of Our Lady of Guadalupe, appeared to a humble Aztec peasant named Juan Diego.

Our Lady of Guadalupe spoke these gentle, tender words of a mother to Juan Diego: "Listen, put it into your heart most little of my children. Let nothing frighten or grieve you. Let not your heart be disturbed. Do not fear any sickness or anguish. Am I not here who am your mother? Are you not under my protection? Am I not your health? Are you not happily within the folds of my mantle, held safely in my arms? Do you need anything more? Let nothing else worry you or disturb you."

Then, as is often the case in Marian apparitions, the Mother of God gave Juan Diego this simple request: she wished that a church be built on the site of her appearance. It is no surprise that Mary asked for a sacred place where her divine Son Jesus could be worshipped and adored. "Mary is a woman of the Eucharist," in the words of Saint John Paul II. She leads us to the Eucharist where we receive the saving mystery of Jesus' Body and Blood as nourishment for the journey of life. Saint John Paul II describes how Mary teaches us to celebrate the Christian mystery when he notes that "at the Annunciation Mary conceived the Son of God in the physical reality of his Body and Blood, thus anticipating within herself what to some degree happens sacramentally in every believer who receives, under the signs of bread and wine, the Lord's Body and Blood" (*Ecclesia de Eucharistia*, 55).

As we continue our journey with the *Catechism*, we find in Mary a loving mother and trusted teacher. As the *Catechism* notes, "in [Mary] the Church admires and exalts the most excellent fruit of redemption and joyfully contemplates, as in a faultless image, that which she herself desires and hopes wholly to be" (1172). This week, as we become alert to the voice of the mother of Jesus, may we hear her tender maternal call to grow in friendship with the Triune God who is Father, Son, and Holy Spirit.

My Journal

Read and reflect on Catechism *1113–1130, 1172–1173.*

Describe the role that Mary plays in your spiritual life. What personal obstacles and challenges do you face, as you seek to grow in devotion to Mary? This week, look for a masterpiece painting, sculpture, mosaic, or stained glass image of Mary that speaks to your heart and mind. You might find this image online or in a book, or perhaps you have access to a church that contains beautiful images of Mary. Spend some time before that image and let it be part of your prayer time this week. If you can, set aside time this week to pray the Rosary, reflecting on Mary's life and example of faith.

WEEK 43

MARY: EXEMPLARY MODEL
OF HOLINESS

LIVE

One frequently heard argument against Christianity is the claim that no one can possibly live up to all of the many demands of the Christian moral life. The idea is that if moral perfection is impossible for human beings to undertake, then the beliefs that inspire morality cannot be taken seriously. God is seen as a severe, demanding, abstract ideal who places on the shoulders of human beings the cruel burden of living by moral guidelines that can never be fully attained. One is left alone, like a frightened child in a dark room, with impossibly burdensome human codes of conduct and little help or guidance for living those moral demands. The only option in this scenario is to avoid the faith that underlies the Christian moral path.

Perhaps you've heard this claim against Christianity before, articulated by a great thinker or someone you know, a family member, a neighbor, a coworker, or a friend. As we continue our journey with the *Catechism*, this week we take a closer look at this assessment of Christianity, and consider the vital part that Mary, Mother of God, plays in our striving to live a morally good life. Mary perfectly demonstrates that the Christian moral life, while demanding, is amazingly livable. Moral goodness and holiness are truly possible for all of us.

Granted, there are some partial truths embedded in the critique of Christian morality. First, the argument rightly assumes the Christian moral life is not easy. It requires courage, discipline, and perseverance to continually direct one's life on a morally good path. A certain determination to "enter through the narrow gate" is needed (Mt 7:13). Perhaps this is why Jesus reminds his listeners often that being his disciple is not easy. Christians are not naïve when it comes to their own moral reality and the moral condition of the world. We know well from experience that good and evil exist. We are aware that the moral life is a constant and, at times, painful struggle between opposing forces.

Second, the argument assumes correctly that our beliefs and way of life should match. In professing a creed, one's life should reflect and embody what is believed in faith. This is certainly true of any religious tradition, and it is especially true of the Catholic Faith. Striving to live by God's laws and the moral wisdom of the Church is a lived expression of faith, not blind submission to harsh, unreachable rules. The moral life flows from what we believe in faith; morality is the Creed lived out.

However, the notion that Christianity is unapproachable because few live up to the Christian way of life is rooted in an idea of God and the divine-human relationship that is not Christian. For the God revealed in the biblical narratives of the Old and New Testaments is a divine person, not an abstract ideal who spews out an impracticable moral code and then watches from afar as humanity fails repeatedly to live by it. Our God is not capricious or cruel; instead, he wishes to live in friendship with us, and that is the whole point of the moral code he gives us.

Divine love calls forth a way of life in keeping with our deepest longings and the eternal meaning and purpose of our lives. Mary, the Mother of God, experienced this divine love at work perfectly in her life. In calling her to be the mother of his Son and our mother, God reveals his divine heart of fatherly love, which is at the core of our call to moral goodness.

Jesus, in his divine person and his own example, to the point of death on a cross, reveals love as the perfection and the fulfillment of the moral law (cf. Rom 13:10). By his life, death, and resurrection, Jesus shows that the path of moral goodness is more about becoming a son or daughter of God, and less about blind obedience to burdensome rules. Moreover, we have the assurance of divine strength to empower us on the path of moral goodness. This we call grace, that is the divine help and strength of the indwelling Holy Spirit given to any disciple of Jesus who strives to live a morally good life. In other words, we are not left alone with moral ideals and unrealistic expectations to struggle with in our weak humanity. We have a heavenly Father who loves us, and who has given us Mary as our mother, to walk with us and help us in our struggle to live as God calls us to live.

We are never alone or without help on our moral journey, fraught as it is with human weakness, failure, and sin.

WALKING WITH THE *CATECHISM*

"From the Church [the Christian] learns the example of holiness and recognizes its model and source in the all-holy Virgin Mary." (2030)

The *Catechism* describes grace as "the help God gives us to respond to our vocation of becoming his adopted sons. It introduces us into the intimacy of the Trinitarian life" (2021). This grace, or divine help, accompanies our striving to live the demands of the Christian life. And the Church presents Mary, Mother of God, as the model, source, and example of holiness and Christian discipleship. Mary is the model, *par excellence*, of holiness and virtue. Why?

God chose Mary to bear his Son into the world. Jesus was born of the Virgin Mary, and his divine humanity was formed by the love and maternal care of his earthly mother. When the Holy Spirit overshadowed Mary at the Annunciation, she became the God-bearer who bore the Son of God into the world. During his earthly life, no one had a closer physical bond with Jesus than his mother. Here's how the *Catechism* puts it: "Mary's role in the Church is inseparable from her union with Christ and flows directly from it. 'This union of the mother with the Son in the work of salvation is made manifest from the time of Christ's virginal conception up to his death'; it is made manifest above all at the hour of his Passion" (964).

So how is Mary an example of holiness to each of us? Does her sinlessness make her an unrealistic ideal or unapproachable as a model of the Christian way of life?

Mary did not earn or merit her state of sinlessness as a reward for something she did. She was conceived without stain of Original Sin because of God's love for her. God set her apart for a unique closeness to his Son Jesus in the power of the Holy Spirit. Mary's holiness comes from her closeness to Jesus. And she shows us, by her life recorded in the Gospels, that our holiness and striving for moral goodness come from remaining close to Jesus in his word and in the sacraments.

Mary, mother of Jesus, draws us into the fullness of life with her Son. She is our spiritual mother who walks with us as a model of holiness. Mary is our mother in the order of grace, as the *Catechism* notes (968). The example of Mary's faith shows us that holiness is not an unattainable ideal but the divine path of grace unique to our lives. By grace, God's life and presence can grow in me, just as Mary bore the Son of God in her heart, mind, and body. Preserved by God from the stain of Original Sin from her conception, Mary teaches us that holiness means becoming a living reflection of Christ in the world.

Looking to her example and relying on God's grace restores our confidence to walk in the ways of God. This is the great adventure of the Christian moral life!

My Journal
Read and reflect on Catechism *1996–2005.*

This week, continue praying the Rosary. In prayer, ask Mary for the grace you need to live the Christian moral life, particularly in areas of weakness. Perhaps you struggle with a habit of impatience, a short temper, laziness, or another moral weakness. In your journal this week, write down at least three ways in which Mary's example helps you persevere in Christian living. As you reflect on the *Catechism*'s teaching on grace, consider whether you rely on your own efforts and strength to grow in holiness. Ask Mary to help you lean with greater trust on the help of God's grace, in the word of God and in the sacraments.

WEEK 44

MARY: EXEMPLARY MODEL
OF PRAYER

PRAY

Our spiritual life is a journey, as is life itself. From birth through death, we experience life as a pilgrimage. And few works of literature capture this fundamental truth of human existence as well as the *Divine Comedy* by the Italian poet Dante Alighieri. Dante began his epic poem, considered one of the greatest works of literature, around 1308 and completed it in 1321, the year of his death. Perhaps you've read the *Divine Comedy*, in full or in parts. Or maybe you're not familiar with it at all. This week's reflection is relevant no matter how much or how little you know of this classic work, for we'll draw on one theme from Dante's journey: Mary, the Mother of God, in her unique role in salvation history and in our spiritual journey.

Dante's journey begins on the night before Good Friday in the year 1300. At the outset, he describes himself as halfway along life's path, lost in a dark wood, attacked by wild beasts, and unable to find direction. To find the right path, the poet sets out on a journey through three realms that divide the poem's three parts: *Inferno, Purgatorio*, and *Paradiso*. Dante's arduous pilgrimage comes to an end with a vision that transforms his longing and his will by "the Love that moves the sun and the other stars" (*Paradiso*, 33.145). As with any spiritual journey, Dante is accompanied by several guides along the way — from the poet Virgil to many saints, to Beatrice, the woman he loved. And when Dante encounters Christ in Paradise, he is accompanied by Mary, who is honored as Queen of the Angels and the Saints.

This detail is important, as Dante is pointing us to a profound truth of our spiritual life. Grace comes through the hands of Mary, the mother of Jesus. This role is given to Mary, not by the saints or those devoted to her intercession, but by God. God himself has given Mary her unique role in the unfolding divine plan to reconcile humanity to his friendship. Mary is the most graced of all creatures, expressed in the Annunciation greeting of the Archangel Gabriel, "Hail, full of grace!" If Mary had not accepted the angel's message, the Son of God could not have taken human flesh to open the gates of heaven by his suffering and death on the cross. The salvation of the world hung on Mary's humble "yes" to God, her obedient *fiat* that reversed the "no," the disobedience of Eve.

For this reason, Dante places Mary at the most elevated place in the celestial realm, surrounded by the love and devotion of the saints and angels. Mary is the new Eve, as the early Church Fathers saw her, whose whole being was offered to God in faith. In one of the most exquisite lines of his poem, Dante tells us why Mary's words in her *fiat* and the *Magnificat* are the pattern and model of the prayer of every Christian:

> Look now on that face that most resembles that of Christ;
> its brightness alone can dispose you to see Christ. (*Paradiso*,
> 32.85–87)

WALKING WITH THE *CATECHISM*

"The prayers of the Virgin Mary, in her Fiat and Magnificat, are characterized by the generous offering of her whole being in faith." (2622)

The Gospels give no individual details or personality description of Mary, such as her age or her physical appearance. What we do know about Mary comes to us in the form of two prayers, one spoken before the Archangel Gabriel and the other before Elizabeth, her cousin. This tells us a lot about the woman God set apart to be the mother of his Son, Jesus. The prayers of Mary, her *Fiat* and her *Magnificat*, summarize all we need to know about her person and her life, for prayer was at the heart of who Mary was.

As our journey with the *Catechism* continues, we focus our reflection this week on these two prayers spoken by Mary, recorded in the Gospels. In Mary's response to the Archangel Gabriel, her *fiat*, we hear Mary's "yes" to God's plan, choosing to fill her with grace and call her to be the mother of his Son, Jesus. In Mary's *Magnificat*, we hear the humble Mother of God praising God for his great deeds.

Mary's "yes" to God was not mindless submission to a gender-bound role, as some argue. Rather, Mary points to her Son, Jesus, and shows the path of true Christian discipleship: humble openness to God's word and presence in our lives. In Mary we see the pattern of our joyful acceptance of our high calling, our vocation to become the reflections of Christ in the world — that is, to become saints! Mary teaches the Church and each one of us how to grow in friendship with God as disciples of her Son, Jesus.

In making the prayers of Mary your own prayers, you will find the meaning and vocation of your life. God calls you by name, just as he called Mary, and he invites you also to respond with a generous "yes." Mary walks with you on the journey of life, through all the ups and downs, and every step of the way!

MY JOURNAL
Read and reflect on Catechism *2673–2682 and Luke 1:26–56.*

Set aside time this week to read Mary's two prayers, recorded in the Gospel of Luke. In particular, pray the *Magnificat* (Lk 1:46–56), slowly and meditatively. Reflect on the traditional prayer of the Hail Mary as described in the *Catechism*. In your journal, write down three virtues that you have learned from Mary's prayers. How will those virtues help you in your daily spiritual journey? (If you have time, read some lines of Canto 23, *Paradiso*, in the *Divine Comedy*, where Christ and Mary appear in Dante's vision of Paradise.)

PART XII

THE COMMUNION OF SAINTS

UNITY OF FAITH

BELIEVE

"This is the greatest week in the history of the world since creation!" said President Richard Nixon as he greeted the Apollo 11 crew on their return from the moon. More than fifty years later, his words may seem like an overstatement, but they certainly capture the excitement and euphoria following one of the greatest human achievements of the twentieth century: space exploration and travel to the moon and back.

While the moon landing was a technological triumph for America, it also marked a rare moment of unity for the entire human race. Astronauts Neil Armstrong and Buzz Aldrin spoke about this special feeling of global unity as they took their first steps on the moon. They also encountered this feeling of universal harmony in peoples around the world who took common pride in this human accomplishment. In that one special moment in time, humanity forgot the many and awful things that divide us as they looked up together at the heavens. And what they saw together was the moon, a single celestial object shared by a common humanity. As Neil Armstrong famously said as he began his historic walk on the moon's surface, "That's one small step for man, one giant leap for mankind."

Moments of great human achievement bring people together, transcending differences of language, culture, and geography. But as we know too well, these moments of global unity are rare and fleeting as we return quickly to all the things that divide us in wars, violence, and injustice. Now, more than fifty years after the first moon landing, the most advanced scientific and technological human achievements fail to overcome the entrenched divisions and polarizations in our society.

Yet there is good news. The Catholic tradition reveals the powerful unity of faith across the diversity of peoples and times in the communion of saints. This communion transcends the human differences of language, culture, and race, with God as the source and sustainer of our unity. By virtue of our baptism, as members of the Church, we belong to the communion of saints, which is made possible in the spiritual unity of the Body of Christ.

The *Catechism* teaches us that we can experience this spiritual reality of the communion of saints at any moment, even in the ordinary moments of our day, not just in historic moments shared by humanity. People from every land, language, race, and culture are members of the communion of saints, and this communion also transcends time and space. All the saints in heaven, the souls in purgatory, and the faithful on earth belong to this communion.

WALKING WITH THE *CATECHISM*
"The Church is a 'communion of saints.'" (960)

We associate the word "church" with religious institutions. Most religions and faith traditions have some form of institutional structure to organize their members. In the Catholic tradition, we believe that beneath and beyond the visible structure of the Church there is a fundamental spiritual reality that makes and holds the community of believers together. The Church is composed of visible parts in the hierarchy, the consecrated or religious life, and the laity. Yet her innermost reality is revealed at a much deeper level than the external, visible structures. The Church is a mystery flowing from the wounded side of Christ on the cross. In faith we see and experience the Church in her most fundamental essence, as the mystery of Christ's continuing presence among all peoples in every age and time.

In the Apostles' Creed, we profess the words, "one, holy, catholic, and apostolic Church." (You can find the *Catechism*'s summary of this article of faith in paragraphs 811–870.) The one Church, founded by Jesus Christ and sustained by the continued outpouring of the Holy Spirit, brings about the communion of the faithful and joins each believer to Christ, the foundation and source of the Church's unity. "After confessing 'the holy catholic Church,' the Apostles' Creed adds 'the communion of saints.' In a certain sense this article is a further explanation of the preceding: 'What is the Church if not the assembly of all the saints?' The communion of saints is the Church" (946).

"The term 'communion of saints' therefore has two closely linked meanings: communion 'in holy things (*sancta*)' and 'among holy persons (*sancti*)'" (948). Baptism incorporates us into the Church as a "communion of saints." Through baptism, we share in the faith of the Church that extends into the past, the present, and the future. Through baptism, we share in the holy things of the Church, most especially the Eucharist, which represents and brings about a marvelous unity of believers across time and space. The "Amen" we pray at every Eucharist joins our single voice with the multiplicity of voices of believers across centuries and cultures. This is a powerful unity of humanity brought about by Jesus Christ and realized in faith!

The term "communion of saints" refers also to the unity we share with holy persons. Saints are living reflections of the face of Christ in the world. God makes saints, the Church simply recognizes the unique holiness of some men and women through the ages by canonizing them. Many saints of the Church may simply be the "next-door saints" that are part of your life. Each saint, known and unknown, reflects virtues and gifts that embody their closeness to Christ. Because of this closeness, the saints are able to help us in our weakness and needs by their intercession to Christ on our behalf. Within the communion of saints, we experience a powerful unity of faith that transcends time, culture, and space. The saints are God's great masterpieces, and you are called to be one of them!

MY JOURNAL
Read and reflect on Catechism 946–962.

Take time this week to reflect on the invitation and privilege of belonging to the communion of saints. In your journal, jot down three ways you can respond to the universal call to holiness in your particular state and stage of life. Recall moments when you have experienced the unity of faith within the community of believers. How were those moments of grace? Take time to read about one canonized saint, whether it's your name saint, your Confirmation saint, the saint of the day, or a saint whose life story inspires you or whose intercession you seek. Find a prayer to pray to that saint each day of this week.

A SPIRITUAL TREASURY

CELEBRATE

Treasure hunts are the subject of many children's games, books, plays, and films. Even adults enjoy a good treasure hunt, as evidenced in popular television game shows and reality survival programs. The thrill of searching for and discovering clues while overcoming obstacles to find a hidden treasure is compelling to our human imagination. We're willing to risk the ride of a treasure hunt in the hope that things will work out in a happy ending, the discovery of some precious, worthwhile prize.

A recent movie that highlighted the thrill of a treasure hunt was *Ready Player One*, a futuristic film based on a book by Ernest Cline. The movie is set in the year 2045, when young people seeking to escape the drudgery of a postapocalyptic society lose themselves in a virtual reality world known as OASIS. The movie follows millions of teenagers who are absorbed in a treasure hunt to discover an Easter egg hidden in one of the virtual worlds. The winner of the treasure hunt is expected to walk away with the personal fortune of the creator of OASIS and inherit the virtual reality world itself. Two teens, the film's central characters, discover the creator's love of 1980s trivia and games as they follow hidden clues leading to the prize. In the process, they also discover how to build up their fragmented world through the friendship that develops during the treasure hunt.

The spiritual life abounds in treasures — not material or earthly goods, but supernatural gifts that come from the hand of a loving and generous God. Yet do we recognize the treasures of the spiritual life?

From the word of God and participation in the Church's sacramental life, we learn that God desires to share with us spiritual treasures that are invisible, yet real. Do we recognize these spiritual gifts and seek after them?

Growing in awareness of our participation in the communion of saints opens us to spiritual goods that flow from Jesus Christ, his Blessed Mother, and the saints in heaven and on earth. Once again we are reminded that we are not alone on our spiritual journey. In the words of the *Catechism*, "The Christian who seeks to purify himself of his sin and to become holy with the help of God's grace is not alone. 'The life of each of God's children is joined in Christ and through Christ in a wonderful way to the life of all the other Christian brethren in the supernatural unity of the Mystical Body of Christ'" (1474).

We are not alone through the ups and downs of life, and this knowledge should give us strength and consolation. Countless spiritual gifts and treasures flow from the communion of saints. When we take stock of all that we long for, search for, and value in life, we can better orient our desires and longings toward God. Friendship and union with God is the "pearl of great price" (Mt 13:46), the precious spiritual treasure we ultimately seek.

WALKING WITH THE CATECHISM

"We also call these spiritual goods of the communion of saints the Church's treasury, *which is 'not the sum total of the material goods which have accumulated during the course of the centuries. On the contrary the "treasury of the Church" is the infinite value ... which Christ's merits have before God.'" (1476)*

Baptism introduces us into the communion of saints. While we are able to know those in our faith community, whether it's the members of the local parish or a small faith group, we may not always be aware of those who journey with us in the communion of saints. Our reflections on the *Catechism* this week invite us to grow in awareness of the many spiritual companions and fellow travelers we can turn to as companions in the spiritual life.

The *Catechism* sums up the communion of saints as "the communion of all the faithful of Christ, those who are pilgrims on earth, the dead who are being purified, and the blessed in heaven, all together forming one Church; and we believe that in this communion, the merciful love of God and his saints is always [attentive] to our prayers" (962).

So what spiritual treasures can we hope for? The *Catechism* points to the Paschal Mystery of Jesus' life, death, and resurrection as the central spiritual treasure that God desired to give us in sending his only Son into the world (1476). The lives of Mary and the saints provide examples of holiness that open the path to countless spiritual riches. Other spiritual treasures of the Church include the poor and the marginalized, who call us out of ourselves in compassion and care; the word of God; and the sacraments of the Church. God's holy word and sacramental presence are spiritual treasures to be discovered again and again at every moment of the day.

Finally, among the many spiritual treasures we discover on the path of faith is the simple awareness of God's love and presence in the ordinary, daily moments of life. God desires your friendship. Recognizing and responding to God's desire to be close to you, to walk with you in the joys and difficulties of life, can be a spiritual treasure hunt you embark on every day!

MY JOURNAL
Read and reflect on Catechism *1474–1477.*

In your journal this week, write down three "treasures" you look for in life. Do these "treasures" lead you closer to or away from God? List spiritual gifts and graces you need at this time on your journey of faith. Perhaps it is peace of mind in God's will, restored relationships with God or family, or a sense of hope and trust in God rather than doubt, anxiety, or despair. Make a concrete plan to help you persevere in reading God's word and participating in the Eucharist. Pray for the intercession and help of the Blessed Virgin Mary and the saints on earth and in heaven to guide you to discover the particular spiritual treasures you need today.

WEEK 47
FINDING TRUE HAPPINESS IN GOD

LIVE

Beginning in the fifteenth century, individual artists began to recover the ancient practice of signing artistic works. As art patronage expanded beyond state and church to include wealthy individuals and families, Renaissance artists sought to draw attention to their distinct artistic talents and secure lucrative commissions and new patrons by stamping their identities on their works. The increased competition of the marketplace drove artists to highlight their individual artistic genius.

The practice of signing a work of art was not common in the eras before the Renaissance — that is the early Christian, Romanesque, Byzantine, and Middle Ages. In the medieval world, sacred art was produced largely by communities of artists who worked in cooperative guilds. Many treasured medieval illuminated manuscripts are known only by the names of their patrons and owners, not the artists and monk scribes who created them. And the same was true of the breathtaking medieval Gothic cathedrals created from the twelfth through the fourteenth centuries, including such masterpieces as Chartres Cathedral. These extraordinary, sacred spaces were the work of architects, sculptors, woodworkers, and stained glass artists who remained anonymous. The medieval world had no need to identify their artists and craftsmen through individual signatures. The focus of their communal effort was to build sacred spaces for the praise and worship of God and to honor the Blessed Virgin Mary and the saints. As an expression of faith and love of

God, the ordinary medieval townsfolk offered their artistic skill and labors to build their magnificent cathedrals over the decades and centuries it took to complete them.

The anonymity of medieval artists might seem strange, even offensive, to our highly self-referential and individualistic worldview. We might rightly criticize the medieval anonymity of artists as an unjust exploitation of labor. We like to receive credit for our achievements, small and great. In a world that places high value on the individual and his or her self-expression, it is unthinkable for an artist not to sign his or her work! But could we learn something of value from the medieval emphasis on the community within which the individual finds his or her roots and identity? The artists and craftsmen of the Middle Ages believed that the glory of their human achievement was to be found in God, not in themselves. Since their skills and labors were being offered to God and for the good of the community, they saw no need for individual fame or recognition. How different this is from our contemporary way of thinking!

How do we approach our daily work, great and small? Do we seek to be valued, appreciated, and recognized for our individual contributions, both in our community of faith and in society? When a family member, a boss, or a coworker does not acknowledge or show appreciation, do we become demoralized and resentful or feel taken for granted?

The *Catechism* reminds us to place our desire for happiness and the natural human longing for esteem, recognition, and appreciation within the invitation to love God above all else. When we feel anonymous, our gaze should move, not inward to the self, but upward to God, who is the source of all our talents, efforts, and achievements. In looking to God as the source of all that is good and praiseworthy in us, we receive the grace, strength, and vision to continue building the masterpiece that is our life.

WALKING WITH THE *CATECHISM*

"True happiness is not found in riches or well-being, in human fame or power, or in any human achievement — however beneficial it may be — such as science, technology, and art, or indeed in any creature, but in God alone, the source of every good and of all love." (1723)

Your journey with the *Catechism* as guide began with reflection on the deepest human longings for happiness, longings shared by all. This natural human desire and search for happiness is of divine origin. God places a desire for happiness deep within our hearts in order to draw us to divine love. And only this divine love of the Father, Son, and Holy Spirit can satisfy our human longing for happiness.

As we continue this spiritual journey, take time this week to reflect on the invitation to love God above all else. Is it possible to put the love of God above all the other loves of our lives? This might seem like an impossible task! How have you responded to feeling under-appreciated or being taken for granted at home, at work, in your community? Did that experience serve as an opportunity to see your work as an offering to God, in whose love alone we find our worth, fulfillment, and happiness?

Our basic human longing for happiness can easily drive us to pursue material riches, wellbeing, fame, or power. Yet this search will fail to satisfy our deepest human longings for love and goodness. As Saint Thomas Aquinas once wrote, "God alone satisfies." (1718).

MY JOURNAL

Read and reflect on Catechism *1716–1728.*

This week we reflect on the dignity, purpose, and value of work in light of our relationship to God. Reflect on those who support and encourage your work and even those who underappreciate your work in the various relationships that make up your daily life. How do you respond to this experience — with gratitude, disillusionment, or resentment? Reflect on and jot down your response to this question: How am I to love God above all else? Identify persons and things that draw you closer to God's love and those that distract you from finding happiness in God alone. Pray for the grace to begin to make this truth of Christian faith a daily reality in your life: God alone satisfies!

SAINTS AS GOD'S MASTERPIECES

PRAY

Eric Lidell was a Scottish Olympic gold medalist whose journey inspired the Oscar-winning movie *Chariots of Fire*. Throughout his experience of training for and racing in the Olympics, Lidell kept a profound spiritual approach to his gift as a world-class athlete. He was known to have said, "I believe God made me for a purpose, but he also made me fast. And when I run I feel his pleasure."

After his Olympic victory, Lidell continued to maintain a spiritual perspective on his remarkable athletic achievement. The celebrity and fame that came with being an Olympic gold medalist did not change or corrupt him. Instead, Olympic success confirmed his lifelong desire to bring the Gospel to those in need. On his return to Scotland, after winning two medals at the 1924 Olympic Games in Paris, he said, "It has been a wonderful experience to compete in the Olympic Games and to bring home a gold medal. But since I have been a young lad, I have had my eyes on a different prize. You see, each one of us is in a greater race than any I have run in Paris, and this race ends when God gives out the medals." Soon after his Olympic victory, Lidell moved to China to become a missionary and teacher. There he dedicated himself to spreading the Gospel until 1945, when he was imprisoned and died in a Japanese internment camp.

In our celebrity-driven culture, we tend to exalt movie stars, athletes, and billionaire business owners as models of achievement and success. We admire their fame, wealth, good looks, business acumen, or athleticism. Yet such human achievements are only half the prize. Of deeper and more lasting significance is the call to grow in friendship with God. As embodied spirits, we were created with a divine purpose, which is to live in friendship with God. Since God is our origin and destiny, our full human flourishing comes from pursuing our life goals *and* striving to be saints.

In an interview given years before his election to the papacy, the future Pope Benedict XVI observed, "The only really effective apologia for Christianity comes down to two arguments, namely, the *saints* the Church has produced and the *art* which has grown in her womb. Better witness is borne to the Lord by the splendor of holiness and art which have arisen in the community of believers than by the clever excuses which apologetics has come up with to justify the dark sides which, sadly, are so frequent in the Church's human history."

Do we look to the Church's saints and artistic treasures as arguments for faith? How often do we turn to the example, wisdom, and intercession of the saints to accompany us on our journey of faith? This week we'll focus on the place of the saints in the Church and in our spiritual journeys, particularly as trusted guides to prayer and mentors in the spiritual life.

The saints are God's masterpieces and the Church's spiritual heroes. And unlike celebrities who point to themselves and their achievements through carefully crafted marketing plans, a saint is transparent to God's love in the world. God works in the world through particular people in their culture, place, and time. God is the one who makes saints; the Church simply confirms God's power and love at work in their holy lives. The witness of saints is hard to argue with, because in them we glimpse the concrete power of God's radiant love, which overcomes every human weakness and sin. Yes, the saints are the first to admit they are sinners; yet they are also ready to do God's will above all else and to trust in the help of God's grace to face the struggles of life.

For these reasons, the Church, from the very beginning, has offered the witness of thousands of holy men and women. These living examples of holiness show us how we can become friends of God in spite of our weaknesses, obstacles, and even the barriers culture might throw in our way.

WALKING WITH THE *CATECHISM*

"The witnesses who have preceded us into the kingdom, especially those whom the Church recognizes as saints, share in the living tradition of

prayer by the example of their lives, the transmission of their writings, and their prayer today." (2683)

The Catholic tradition of turning to the saints as models of holiness and intercessors in prayer is a stumbling block for many. Does giving the saints a place in our spiritual life and approaching God through their intercession lead to idolatry of human beings?

The spiritual practice of turning to the saints as models and guides to prayer is rooted in the firm conviction that the lives of holy men and women are not ends in themselves. Rather they are guides to virtue and prayer who point the way to God in concrete, tangible ways. Just as a GPS helps us find our destination, the transfigured lives of these spiritual guides lead us to God, our final spiritual destination. In practical ways, the saints show us how to deepen prayer and grow in faith, hope, and love. We imitate their example and rely on their spiritual aid.

The saints make the spiritual life real and accessible. They remind us that it is possible to make God the center and priority of our lives. They prompt us to measure our best achievements and worst failures against our response to God's call to holiness. By their lived example of holiness and their prayers for us, the saints show us how to become the kind of person who can live with God forever. They teach us how to live in radical obedience to God's will and in confident trust that God's grace is sufficient to overcome adversity and malice. Most of all, the saints radiate love of God and love of neighbor, particularly love of the poor and forgotten. As they stayed close to God in prayer during their earthly life, the saints continue to remain close to God in eternal life. For these reasons we turn to them as spiritual guides.

The *Catechism* reminds us of the role the saints have in our spiritual life. We can draw on the wisdom of the saints to grow in prayerful union with God, for the saints "contemplate God, praise him and constantly care for those whom they have left on earth. ... Their intercession is their most exalted service to God's plan. We can and should ask them to intercede for us and for the whole world" (2683).

My Journal
Read and reflect on Catechism *2683–2691.*

Reflect on your understanding of the saints and the place they
have in your spiritual life. Take time this week to write down questions or obstacles you face in praying to God through the intercession of the saints. From the vast treasury of saints of the Church,
choose one saint you are drawn to at this particular time in your
life. If they have writings, plan to read them for a few minutes each
day this week. Ask the saint to intercede on your behalf to God
and look for the concrete ways he or she can help you grow as a
friend of God.

PART XIII

DAILY CONVERSION

WEEK 49
LIFE'S FINAL GOAL

BELIEVE

The Last Judgment took Michelangelo over four years to complete. The monumental fresco was finished in 1541, including some 300 muscular figures gathered in tumultuous, swirling motion around the central and powerful figure of Christ, with Mary close at his side. Christ appears at the ultimate moment of truth, when the faithful are joined to him in the bliss of eternal union with God and the corrupt are cast into endless separation from God. The artist's majestic vision of the end of time carried to a dramatic close the biblical narrative cycle he had begun on the Sistine ceiling with the creation of Adam and Eve. In depicting the anticipated, yet dreaded, moment of Christ's judgment of the world, Michelangelo translated into the grandest visual form the words of the Creed: "I believe in the resurrection of the body and life everlasting."

Your journey with the *Catechism* as guide began with a reflection on the human longing for God. But where does this desire for God come from? It is inscribed deep in each human heart, created by God and for God. And God never stops drawing us to himself. The high dignity and inestimable worth of every human being rests on this spiritual reality: from the first moment of our existence, we are called to communion with God, now and for all eternity.

Father James Schall, SJ, noted that Eric Voegelin, a twentieth-century philosopher and professor, often told his students that they acted in daily life as if they had an ultimate meaning and purpose beyond this life. To the surprise of his agnostic and atheist students, he reminded them that they acted as if they were immortal! Our most ordinary human actions in relationships and work assume, in some way or another, that we are immortal. Pause and think about how your ordinary daily activity, at home and at work, aims for fulfillment that will not be found in this life, however long you might live.

Only in God do we find the happiness and truth implicit in all human action and search for fulfillment. The final goal of life is union with God in friendship. In other words, your friendship with God, begun in this life, will continue in the life that is to come. This is why Christians place their hope in God's promise of a new resurrected life, once this earthly life ends. Life on earth is a prelude and preparation for the transfigured, eternal life in the presence of God, who alone satisfies the deepest longings of the human heart.

Before Jesus entered his suffering and death on the cross, he was transfigured before his disciples, Peter, James, and John. At that moment "his face changed in appearance and his clothing became dazzling white" (Lk 9:29). The *Catechism* tells us that Jesus' transfiguration "'is the sacrament of the second regeneration,'" in which we are given "a foretaste of Christ's glorious coming, when he 'will change our lowly body to be like his glorious body'" (556).

Christians believe that the life of the human person continues after death. This week we will reflect on these profound, yet simple questions: When and who will rise from the dead? How can we believe that our body, so clearly mortal, could rise to everlasting life?

WALKING WITH THE *CATECHISM*

"We firmly believe, and hence we hope that, just as Christ is truly risen from the dead and lives forever, so after death the righteous will live for ever with the risen Christ and he will raise them up on the last day. Our resurrection, like his own, will be the work of the Most Holy Trinity." (989)

The *Catechism* tells us, "From the beginning, Christian faith in the resurrection has met with incomprehension and opposition. 'On no point does the Christian faith encounter more opposition than on the resurrection of the body'" (996). This is understandable, since no physical proof or tangible evidence exists for Jesus' resurrection and the resurrection of the human body. It is an article of Christian faith, hope, and love!

How do we come to believe in bodily resurrection? Belief in the resurrection of the body is a consequence of believing that God created each of us out of love as a whole human person, body, mind, and soul. I am not at the origin of my own existence. Only God is. And each day my earthly, bodily existence moves toward God, my creator. Moreover, in baptism, in a certain way we already rise with Christ. We live out the full meaning of our baptism by believing in the future resurrection of our bodies. United with Christ by baptism, we already participate now in the heavenly life of the risen Christ in a life that remains "hidden with Christ in God" (Col 3:3). Nourished by the sacramental food of Christ's own Body and Blood in the Eucharist, we belong, here and now, to the Body of Christ.

So when will the resurrection of the body take place? At the end of time, on the last day. As Saint Paul writes in his first letter to the Thessalonians, "The Lord himself, with a word of command, with the voice of an archangel and with the trumpet of God, will come down from heaven, and the dead in Christ will rise first" (1 Thess 4:16). By the power of his glorious resurrection from the dead, Jesus will raise each one of us in a glorified, "spiritual body." So we return to the question: How can this be? The *Catechism* notes, "This 'how' exceeds our imagination and understanding; it is accessible only to faith. Yet our participation in the Eucharist already gives us a foretaste of Christ's transfiguration of our bodies" (1000).

Michelangelo and countless artists through the ages have attempted to capture that eternal moment when Christ will come again in glory to judge the living and the dead. Their artistic vision invites us to "see" our eternal life with God with eyes of faith.

MY JOURNAL
Read and reflect on Catechism 988–1004.

Set time aside this week to reflect on the article of the Creed, "I believe in the resurrection of the body and life everlasting." Write down your difficulties or doubts in understanding or accepting this article of faith. Pray for the guidance of the Holy Spirit to lead you to understanding and faith. Reflect on the ways in which your baptism and participation in the Eucharist are connected to your belief in the resurrection of the body and eternal life. Jot down concrete examples of your daily actions at home and at work that show how you presume your life is immortal.

WEEK 50
SACRAMENTALS

CELEBRATE

Saint John Paul II is known to the world as a beloved pope, a gifted philosopher and theologian, an engaging communicator, and a tireless pastor of the universal church. Not as well known are the difficult personal struggles the young Karol Wojtyła overcame as he discerned God's call to the priesthood. His first words as pope encouraged the world, "Do not be afraid. Open wide the doors for Christ." He knew firsthand the paralyzing effects of fear, having lived through two of the most fearfully oppressive, destructive ideologies of the twentieth century, namely Nazism and Communism. His vocation to a dedicated life of priestly service unfolded against the backdrop of his personal experience of these fearful totalitarian regimes.

By the age of twenty-one, he found himself with no immediate family, completely alone. He lost his mother to illness when he was eight. Then his older brother, a doctor, died a few years later from scarlet fever contracted from patients. And then, soon after the Nazis marched brutally through his native country of Poland, his father passed away in February, 1941. In his book, *Stories of Karol*, Gian Franco Svidercoschi tells the story of Wojtyła's close and dangerous encounter with the Gestapo on their ruthless sweep of Krakow on "Black Sunday," August 6, 1944. They were looking to arrest all young men in order to prevent an uprising like the Warsaw Uprising, which had broken out a few days earlier. They arrested more than eight thousand men and teenagers, many of whose lives ended in concentration camps.

The menacing sound of Nazi high boots could be heard echoing through the deserted streets of Kraków. The young Karol was about to leave his basement room when he heard the chilling sound. Alone in the house, he froze as SS soldiers stopped in front of his door. His head pounding in extreme fear, Karol "stretched out on the ground, with his arms forming a cross." After what must have felt like an eternity, the soldiers continued on. Karol's life had been spared. He knew then that his life had been spared for a reason. He was to serve the faithful as God's priest in the midst of the dark forces that had overtaken his country.

The Sign of the Cross is one of many sacred signs called "sacramentals" in the Catholic tradition. Instituted by the Church, sacramentals are signs meant to predispose us to receive the sanctifying grace of the sacraments and to bless moments of everyday life. Sacramentals commonly associated with Catholic devotions include blessing prayers, rosaries, medals of saints, holy water, scapulars, and the Sign of the Cross. Taking time to understand sacramentals allows us to appreciate the concrete and tangible signs that point us to the graces of the sacraments, which deepen our friendship with God.

WALKING WITH THE *CATECHISM*

"Sacramentals are sacred signs instituted by the Church. They prepare men to receive the fruit of the sacraments and sanctify different circumstances of life." (1677)

How do sacramentals differ from the seven sacraments of the Church? The seven sacraments of the Church are instituted by Jesus Christ. Each of the sacraments continues in the Church and in our lives the divine grace which flows from the paschal mystery. Through the seven sacraments, Jesus continues to pour out his self-giving, redemptive love for all people and in every age of the Church.

Sacramentals, by contrast, are instituted by the Church. The *Catechism* outlines two main effects of sacramentals: first, to open and to predispose us to the sanctifying grace of the sacraments, and second, to bless and make holy various and ordinary circumstances of life (cf. 1670). The blessing of persons, meals, objects, and places is considered one of the primary sacramentals of the Church. The paschal mystery — Jesus' saving Passion, Death, and Resurrection — is the one source from which the seven sacraments and sacramentals draw their power to bring God's grace into the world (cf. 1670).

Why does the Church institute sacramentals if Jesus already instituted the seven sacraments? Sacramentals never take the place of the sacraments. Their purpose is "to prepare us to receive grace and dispose us to cooperate with it" (1670). Sacramentals "always include a prayer, often accompanied by a specific sign, such as the laying on of hands, the sign of the cross, or the sprinkling of holy water (which recalls baptism)" (1668). The Church imparts these blessings by invoking the name of Jesus, usually accompanied by the Sign of the Cross. Through the presence and use of sacramentals, our every day is brought into the holy presence of God. For by these daily blessings we are able to offer "praise of God for his works and gifts, and the Church's intercession for men that they may be able to use God's gifts according to the spirit of the Gospel" (1678).

The journey of life is filled with joys and challenges. Human weakness and sin are a reality in the world, in the Church, and in us. In the midst of the daily routine of life, sacramentals are sacred signs of transcendence reminding us of the invisible life of the Holy Spirit that is as real as the visible, material, and often daunting world around us.

My Journal

Read and reflect on Catechism *1667–1679.*

Reflect on the place of prayers of blessing in your daily life. Do you pray a blessing before meals, over children, or before important events or times of the day? Are blessing prayers, from Scripture or spontaneously said, part of your everyday routine? Read and reflect on sacramentals such as saints' medals or holy water and their purpose in sanctifying the ordinary moments of each day. Have your sacred objects blessed by a priest during this week.

WEEK 51
THE HABIT OF VIRTUE

LIVE

When a neighbor announced she planned to run a marathon, her inner drive and motivation impressed the community. Even more remarkable was the transformation of her daily habits as she prepared to achieve her goal. In the months leading up to the marathon, she kept to a rigorous running schedule, made changes to her diet, got plenty of rest, and fought through the physical aches and pains that come with intense training routines. Without the discipline required of marathon runners, she would not have accomplished her goal. The more she persevered in good habits, the easier the training became. On race day, she beamed with a sense of accomplishment while noting that every step of the rigorous discipline she had followed for many months was worth the satisfaction of completing the race.

In making this journey with the *Catechism*, you began the adventure of a spiritual discipline. Your perseverance on this journey is rooted in your desire to grow in the spiritual life. You've come to discover that spiritual discipline is a necessary part of the journey of faith. The same is true of the Christian moral life. If we desire to be virtuous (that is, to do good and to be good), we need spiritual discipline.

Striving to be a good or moral person does not require that we never enjoy pleasure or have fun. In fact, the reality of human experience is the opposite. Self-seeking pleasures enslave us, making us less free and more dissatisfied and unhappy with our lives. The *Catechism* places love at the center of the longing to be virtuous as we choose to do and become good. Saint Augustine said it well when he wrote, "To live well is nothing other than to love God with all one's heart, with all one's soul and with all one's efforts" (1809).

Jesus told his followers to strive to enter the kingdom of God "through the narrow gate" (Mt 7:13). Doesn't this image paint a picture of the Christian life as a restrictive, unrealistic burden that few live up to? No! Instead, Jesus is inviting us to the discipline of discipleship, which strengthens us to complete the race that opens the door to eternal life with God. The more our habits are aimed toward the good, the easier the moral life becomes. We were created for eternal union with God, and spiritual discipline is the path to move our lives in the direction of the destination of our souls' journey.

Spiritual discipline, which shapes us into virtuous persons, is never easy. Yet it is the only path leading to inner peace and dependence on God in all circumstances of life. Growing in virtue requires the courage to say "yes" to the good and "no" to that which is not of God. Thus the author of the Letter to the Hebrews reminds us of a truth we know well: "At the time, all discipline seems a cause not for joy but for pain, yet later it brings the peaceful fruit of righteousness to those who are trained by it" (Heb 12:11).

Thankfully, the spiritual discipline that gets us into spiritual shape to choose and to do the good is not driven solely by our own determination and strength. Divine grace is available to us every day to strengthen our efforts to be virtuous persons. So the moral life is not a burden on our lives, but the way in which we share in God's power to bring goodness into the world. Most likely, we will fall off the moral path, and we'll need to pick ourselves up again and again to persevere in forming habits that dispose us to doing and being good. As the *Catechism* notes, "It is not easy for man, wounded by sin, to maintain moral balance. Christ's gift of salvation offers us the grace necessary to persevere in the pursuit of the virtues. Everyone should always ask for this grace of light and strength, frequent the sacraments, cooperate with the Holy Spirit, and follow his calls to love what is good and shun evil" (1811).

Walking with the Catechism

"A virtue is an habitual and firm disposition to do the good. It allows the person not only to perform good acts, but to give the best of himself. The

virtuous person tends toward the good with all his sensory and spiritual
powers; he pursues the good and chooses it in concrete actions." (1803)

The *Catechism* discusses two categories of virtues: cardinal virtues and
theological virtues. The cardinal virtues are prudence, justice, forti-
tude, and temperance. The theological virtues are faith, hope, and love.
This week we will consider spiritual practices the Church offers to help
us become virtuous.

These are some of the practical, daily spiritual disciplines that
strengthen us as we strive to enter through the narrow gate:

- First, making time for God in the midst of our busy day.
  Over time, moments set aside for God become the source
  from which all activities, decisions, and actions flow.
- Second, turning to Scripture in silent, prayerful reflection.
  This practice opens the way for God to speak divine wisdom into the events, joys, and challenges of our lives.
- Third, daily spiritual reading helps deepen our understanding of what we profess in the Creed. Prayerful reflection on
  Scripture and consistent spiritual reading allow the abiding
  presence of the Holy Spirit to shape our thoughts, words,
  and actions to God's loving plan for our lives.
- A fourth spiritual discipline is ongoing and active participation in the Church's sacramental life, by which Jesus continues his saving and healing presence in our lives. By im-
  mersing ourselves in the sacraments, we are able to tap into
  God's grace and power, which breaks through the weakness
  and sinfulness of the human condition.
- A fifth spiritual discipline is dedication to works of charity
  and compassion for the sick and the poor. Care for creation
  and stewardship of the created world also calls me out of
  myself. This practice helps form us in habitual, self-giving
  love so we can become living instruments of God's love to
  those in need.
- Finally, praying for and relying with confidence on God's
  grace to live the virtues every day allows us to share in
  God's power to transform the world with good.

The *Catechism* summarizes these disciplines in this way: "Human virtues acquired by education, by deliberate acts and by a perseverance ever-renewed in repeated efforts are purified and elevated by divine grace. With God's help, they forge character and give facility in the practice of the good. The virtuous man is happy to practice them" (1810).

MY JOURNAL
Read and reflect on Catechism *1803–1845.*

Set aside time this week to read the *Catechism* on the virtues of the Christian life. List two to three virtues that you need in your personal journey of faith in your vocation at this time in your life. During times of prayer this week, ask God to open your heart to receive the graces needed to grow in the virtues you've identified. At the end of the week, jot down one spiritual discipline or spiritual habit you will strive to practice for growth in virtue.
